D1215918

*Interrogating the Language
of "Self" and "Other"
in the History of Modern
Christian Mission*

Missional Church, Public Theology, World Christianity

Stephen Bevans, Paul S. Chung, Veli-Matti Kärkkäinen,
and Craig L. Nessan, Series Editors

IN THE MIDST OF globalization there is crisis as well as opportunity. A model of God's mission is of special significance for ecclesiology and public theology when explored in diverse perspectives and frameworks in the postcolonial context of World Christianity. In the face of the new, complex global civilization characterized by the Second Axial Age, the theology of mission, missional ecclesiology, and public ethics endeavor to provide a larger framework for missiology. It does so in interaction with our social, multicultural, political, economic, and intercivilizational situation. These fields create ways to refurbish mission as constructive theology in critical and creative engagement with cultural anthropology, world religions, prophetic theology, postcolonial hermeneutics, and contextual theologies of World Christianity. Such endeavors play a critical role in generating theological, missional, social-ethical alternatives to the reality of Empire—a reality characterized by civilizational conflict, and by the complex system of a colonized lifeworld that is embedded within practices of greed, dominion, and ecological devastation. This series—Missional Church, Public Theology, World Christianity—invites scholars to promote alternative church practices for life-enhancing culture and for evangelization as telling the truth in the public sphere, especially in solidarity with those on the margins and in ecological stewardship for the lifeworld.

Interrogating the Language of "Self" and "Other" in the History of Modern Christian Mission

Contestation, Subversion, and Re-imagination

Man-Hei Yip

Foreword by Craig L. Nessan

PICKWICK *Publications* · Eugene, Oregon

INTERROGATING THE LANGUAGE OF "SELF" AND "OTHER" IN THE
HISTORY OF MODERN CHRISTIAN MISSION
Contestation, Subversion, and Re-imagination

Missional Church, Public Theology, World Christianity 11

Pickwick Publications
An Imprint of Wipf and Stock Publishers
199 W. 8th Ave., Suite 3
Eugene, OR 97401

www.wipfandstock.com

PAPERBACK ISBN: 978-1-5326-7430-3
HARDCOVER ISBN: 978-1-5326-7431-0
EBOOK ISBN: 978-1-5326-7432-7

Cataloguing-in-Publication data:

Names: Yip, Man-Hei, author. | Nessan, Craig L., foreword.

Title: Interrogating the language of "self" and "other" in the history of modern
christian mission : contestation, subversion, and re-imagination / Man-Hei Yip ;
foreword by Craig L. Nessan.

Description: Eugene, OR : Pickwick Publications, 2020 | Missional Church, Public
Theology, World Christianity 11 | Includes bibliographical references and
index(es).

Identifiers: ISBN 978-1-5326-7430-3 (paperback) | ISBN 978-1-5326-7431-0 (hard-
cover) | ISBN 978-1-5326-7432-7 (ebook)

Subjects: LCSH: Mission of the church. | Missions—History.

Classification: BV2063 .Y59 2020 (print) | BV2063 .Y59 (ebook)

Manufactured in the U.S.A.   JULY 2, 2020

For Ryan

Contents

Foreword

Then Jesus told the disciples a parable on the necessity of praying always and not losing heart: "Once there was a judge in a certain city who feared no one—not even God. A woman in that city who had been widowed kept coming to the judge and saying, 'Give me legal protection from my opponent.' For a time the judge refused, but finally the judge thought, 'I care little for God or people, but this woman will not let me alone. I'd better give her the protection she seeks, or she'll keep coming and wear me out.'" Jesus said: "Listen to what this corrupt judge is saying. Won't God then do justice to the chosen who call out day and night? Will God delay long over them? I tell you, God will give them swift justice. But when the Promised One comes, will faith be found anywhere on earth?" (Luke 18:1–8 The Inclusive New Testament)

THIS BOOK IS ABOUT the persistence, even relentlessness, of those dedicating both their scholarship and their life energy to deconstruct, dismantle, and overcome the structures of colonialism that continue to divide the world and church. Even after decades of postcolonial discourse and practices to implement new ways of relating, the propensity to objectify and thereby disregard "others" plagues our world. Such "othering" is not mere impropriety or political incorrectness. We live at a time when we are witnessing how the prophetic cries warning against categorizing others as "disposable people" in an "age of triage" are being fulfilled. The "othering" of immigrants and refugees in the United States leading to their brutal treatment as a matter of public policy and the crimes against "others" in Russia and China are stunning evidence of a global phenomenon. Despite the formal commitment of the community of nations to the Universal Declaration of Human

Rights, disregard for the basic dignity and legal protections due each person is alarming.

"Language is the house of Being" (Heidegger). If how we think is the origin of what we say, then what we say constructs social worlds. We are called to discipline ourselves in thought, word, and deed. Our social reality begins with how we choose to think about things and how we intentionally speak about things. We have daily evidence for how language is being employed in calculated ways to polarize public discourse and identify scapegoats as a form of social control. The anxiety and fear generated in society inevitably leads to policies that scapegoat identifiable victims, yet these dynamics seem hidden from our awareness (Girard). The Gospel of Jesus Christ, culminating in his crucifixion and resurrection, discloses how scapegoating does its harmful work. Christian people, those who center their faith on Christ crucified and risen, are called to name scapegoating for what it is and to resist for Christ's sake.

Man-Hei Yip makes a significant contribution to reimagining the language of Christian mission, which has been fraught by turning people into "others." She proposes that we deconstruct shopworn assumptions about "reconciliation" and excavate the biblical texts anew. Reconciliation begins with contrition and repentance as the predisposition for entering reconciled relationships. Her insightful interrogation of biblical and theological texts establishes common ground with readers. Becoming versed in a new language about reconciliation through repentance leads to the practice of interpreting the actions of others in the kindest way. This practice is severely challenged in a political climate where others are daily being objectified by aggressive language. While there is a reactive impulse to retaliate in kind, the power of the cross interrupts spirals of violent rhetoric leading to harmful acts. As Man-Hei Yip contends, "Our language will no longer be the language of damnation and domination, but one that embraces difference and diversity."

A new language of mission fosters mutuality, not dependence. This extends not only to inter-Christian discourse but to those of other religions or no religion at all. The conviction by Christians that all people are created in God's image entails infinite respect for the dignity of every person without regard for any qualifying conditions. Special care must be made that those engaged in mission not allow their language to disguise ethnocentric presuppositions that contradict the always life-giving purposes of God. We are invited to be transformed by the language that houses the being of others and learn to live together in the commons created among us. Man-Hei Yip asserts that mission discourse "pays attention to the stories of others" to "foster effective intercultural engagement." The resulting "intersubjectivity" unfolds in ongoing relationships that remain a journey ("on the way") and not a destination. We relate to one another dialogically, analogous to the way of friendship, following the instruction of Jesus to love our neighbors as ourselves. The measure of mission becomes the degree to which we ourselves are transformed by these relationships.

This book is a constructive contribution to the necessary process of reimagining what I have elsewhere called "reciprocating mission." I highly commend this work with its fresh perspectives from a challenging theologian whose voice promises to transform your thought, language, and action.

Craig L. Nessan
Academic Dean and William D. Streng Professor for the Education and Renewal of the Church
Wartburg Theological Seminary
Dubuque, Iowa
Advent 2019

Preface

SEVERAL YEARS AGO, I presented a paper on language and the expansion of Christianity at a mission conference. I questioned the language used in missionary activities and how that might help dichotomize worldviews, demarcates groups, and creates distinctions between us and them. After my presentation, someone came up to me and said all derogatory terms were corrected and dwelling on past mistakes would get us nowhere.

There are people who passionately embrace the progress rhetoric and downplay the history of colonialism and its ensuing impact on indigenous people's life and their cultures. Certainly, there are good things about missionary work; however, there are bad things, too. The latter regularly receive minimal attention. Denial grants an easy access for those who desire to divorce themselves from a reality they do not like, and it is the reality of losing power and control.

If missionary (mis)demeanors have all been "corrected," complaints about missionary practices should have died down. General perceptions of missionary work have not been changed completely. The indigenous or leaders from the Global South continue to speak against misrepresentation and imposition of values. Are mistakes corrected, sincerely?

One may wonder if the "solution" made by mission societies and institutions is able to trickle down into revolutionary changes for missionary practice worldwide. We need also to ask if the language crafted in the discourse rightly and justly speaks to power. Any claim that arbitrarily presumes "optimism" of the missionary movement is involved in a modern form of imperialist brainwashing. Similarly, the thought that past mistakes in missionary activities have all been corrected is no different from policing and regulating the speech. This is appalling when the dissonant voice is allowed but restricted to the level that does not run counter to the myth of progress deposited in the global Christian missionary movement.

Rendering the dissonant voice as outdated, predictable, and lacking creativity is clearly an attempt to coerce the other to speak the same language as the mission societies and agencies speak. This form of coercive behavior aims to wipe out certain individuals' past and histories. By sustaining the kind of discourses that endorse self-glorification in the achievement of missionary work, regulating the speech of the other intensifies the process of Western domestication of the entire Christian missionary movement.

Christian mission cannot rely on a top-down approach that ignores the gifts of Christian witness and other religions from the majority world. Nobody can speak and act for the other. There is no way for "us" to talk about the future of Christian mission, when spreading half-truths about the people continually normalizes missionary practice. Some regions in the world are yet to phase out the colonial status. Countries that have gained independence are still experiencing political instability. When we ignore the impact of colonialism or simply refrain from talking about it, we erase the memories of many who have suffered from colonial hegemony. People of later generations are less likely to be sensitive and sympathetic to the pain of the colonized. Learning from the past, including mistakes and failures, is a viable option to heal and to move forward.

Language and Christian mission intersect in complicated ways to subjugate the other in cross-cultural encounter. While the history of Christian mission is predicated on the construction of otherness, our missiological language fails to evaluate how language as a structure of authority reinforces prejudicial thinking, condones aggressive behaviors, and secures one's dominant role in the field.

This book will first indicate how prevailing mission discourses fall short of addressing power imbalances in relationships. Critical theories are useful tools to help unmask the binarial relations, and contest established ideas of otherness or imperialist discourses that sought to otherize the other. Christian mission turns out a platform for expressing one's individuality devoid of the other's voice, and mission discourses have strengthened such self-centeredness that was even documented in the ecumenical meetings over the centuries.

The task of confronting self-centric motivations becomes particularly relevant concerning the future of Christian missionary movement. Reconstructing self urges us to rethink who we are that further creates a pathway for human flourishing. In the meantime, reconceptualizing otherness is decisive for missiological exploration if the mission enterprise must deliver value to all stakeholders in its undertakings. A more effective way of upholding the dignity of other is to see otherness as gift. The emergent discourse can subvert narrative that continues to fetishize the indigenous as cultural stereotypes. This affirmation represents an incredible game-changer in the missionary movement.

Language in missionary work should always aim to reestablish broken relationships between one and other. This is of vital importance for a world that is dominated by bigoted discourses, lies, and hate speech. Any responsible missiological language should acknowledge the agency of the other, which will eventually materialize a persuasive statement that the other is an active participant in human history. The new language symbolizes an act of resistance to the narrative that divides.

Boston, Massachusetts
2019

Acknowledgments

WRITING A BOOK FROM my doctoral dissertation is harder than I thought, and more rewarding than I could ever imagine. This book could not have been possible without the support, advice, and expertise of a number of wonderful people. First of all, I would like to express my deepest gratitude to J. Paul Rajashekar for his supervision during my doctoral studies. Paul provided a perfect balance of guidance and independence for my work. He inspired me to find my voice in writing. He would unhesitatingly help me to stay focused and on track, throughout the duration of research and writing. I am also deeply indebted to John F. Hoffmeyer, for his constructive feedback on my dissertation manuscript. John extended a great amount of assistance. His comments and questions were insightful that helped widen my research focus.

I am eternally grateful to Craig L. Nessan. Craig is a great mentor. He offered valuable guidance on my journey, in particular the time I spent my formative years in Dubuque, Iowa. He was tremendously supportive. He identified the sources of support for connection in doctoral program, and he introduced me to Matthew Wimer of Wipf and Stock Publishers. Matt is friendly and easy to work with. I thank him for helping to bring this work into publication under the Pickwick Publications imprint.

My special thanks go to Rev. Margaret Payne, former bishop of the New England Synod of the Evangelical Lutheran Church in America (ELCA). Thank you for reading my multiple drafts and sending me helpful editing notes.

Last but not least, I owe a huge debt of gratitude to my husband for his immense support, love, and patience over the years. Because of his caring and thoughtfulness, I am able to follow my dream without worrying about failure too much. He is always the one I could turn to during the ups and downs. I am so thankful and blessed to have these people in my life. You make me a better person. Thank you for all the meaningful conversations and shared memories.

1

Introduction

> Colonialists often discursively constructed contrastive para-
> digms such as Christian/savage, civilized/barbaric and orderly/
> disorderly in order to define themselves, and also to explain the
> dominance and acceleration of colonial rule. Such contrastive
> pairings helped to condemn the other as inferior and also helped
> to determine the nature of their hold over the people they subju-
> gated. The early missionary hermeneutics which abetted in this
> enterprise extrapolated this binary view to inject its own biblical
> values into the private and public lives of the colonized.[1]

WHAT CAUSES EASY DICHOTOMIZATION of us and them upon missionary
encounter? Is conflict between civilizations unavoidable?[2] Problematizing
otherness upon missionary encounter is a common tactic to deal with the
other. The problem of othering is closely linked with language use. Prevailing
mission discourses and theological conceptions largely operate within the
Anglo-European cultural and linguistic frameworks. Whether they effectively use words to influence people or negatively construe and describe
people, language becomes a matter of practical concern. The resulting behavior is seemingly external. Language and the Christian missionary movement intersect in complicated ways to objectify the other in cross-cultural
situations. The history of Christian mission has long been predicated on
the construction of otherness. Simply banning the use of certain words and
replacing them by more inclusive language does not address the issue.

---

1. R. S. Sugirtharajah argues that early missionaries might not be involved in colonial administration, but they helped promote and reinforce "perceptions of colonialism" through biblical interpretation and teaching. Sugirtharajah, *Bible and the Third
World*, 62.

2. Huntington, "Clash of Civilizations?," 22.

1

There is, however, not much discussion regarding language use in the Christian missionary movement. It always baffles me when the ecumenical circles embrace the principles of mutuality; the respect paid to the other unfortunately functions to fix the problem of the other. It is my desire to contest a certain account of missiological argument, rationality, and deliberation that have been approved to implement divisive practices. Questioning the decision-making process involves an interrogation of epistemology deployed in the study of the other. It means to disrupt the norm of crafting mission discourses in established structures and linguistic traditions. My contention is that rethinking otherness is necessary for every missionary endeavor. Otherness cannot be treated as an end that justifies the means. Otherness is a manifestation of God's grace and faithfulness to the world. The discourse of otherness as gift becomes a point of departure that subverts the foundational predisposition to see self as better than other.

The task of unearthing otherness opens up a larger question concerning the agency of the other. The issue of full personhood is a serious business. It goes beyond empowering the unfortunate, to recognizing the value of the other. Who are these people? What does it mean to recognize their value? To what extent will the ecumenical body tolerate otherness and allow that to instigate institutional change? I am asking these questions, not because I can give a better answer than anyone else. I am inviting all of us to reflect on this significant topic concerning the intersubjective reality of Christian missionary engagement. Renewing our approach to language can build positive relationships, which will in turn shed light on the discipline of missiology.

A Methodological Problem

In this chapter, I will first examine the problems that arise from overemphasizing achievements of mission agencies and societies. Then I will proceed to the need of a new methodology that attempts to address linguistic issues in relation to the construction of otherness in Christian missionary movement.

Bias in Historical Interpretation: Privatization of Knowledge and Religion

The study of Christian mission has given prominence to a framework that focuses almost exclusively on the major player whose agenda and decision are shaping mission strategy and missionary work. Traditionally, mission agencies and societies have assumed a role of the agent of God bringing God's salvation to the ends of the world. They also could effectively amass the most needed resources including monetary means and technological know-how. They are the doer or deliverer of missionary work. When the doer of historical events possesses and presents a better access to knowledge than anybody else, that knowledge embedded in missionary work is perceived as a given. That knowledge provides the underlying basis for why we do what we do in the missionary movement. A methodology that is situated at the agencies' vantage point easily speaks a language in their best interests. Given the self-centric approach, there is a consequential preservation of bias toward self versus the other.

Receivers of mission are given little space to negotiate their identities in the daily operation of salvation-related programs. They are largely reduced to a homogeneous group, waiting to be empowered. Interestingly, these people came to be known as people of the Third World. The term "Third World" is a modern term popularized in the early 1950s to refer to the countries of Africa, Asia, and Latin America.[3] Images of the Third World were mostly deplorable, as soon as the term came into usage. According to Ernest W. Lefever,

> Most Third World states have pluralistic societies made up of several, and sometimes many, racial, ethnic, and religious groups, frequently in rivalry or conflict with one another. Their governments tend to be weak and fragile and are often dominated by a privileged class or ethnic group. Most such regimes are authoritarian, and their leaders, seeking to maintain themselves in power and to modernize simultaneously, guarantee few of the political and civil rights taken for granted in the democratic West.[4]

What Lefever illustrated is a negative construct of the people who are relative to the West and possibly at odds with the West.[5] Problems occur when people interpret history through a single lens, and make universal claims on the basis of their interpretation of the world and the other. That

---

3. Lefever, *Amsterdam to Nairobi*, 7. The term "Third World" in its original French usage, *tiers monde*, refers to an alternative world that distinguishes itself from the capitalist world (first world) and the socialist world (second world). It is not necessarily associated with a hierarchical order in which first is the most superior and third is the least significant. Scott and Cavanaugh, *Blackwell Companion to Political Theology*, 257.

4. Lefever, *Amsterdam to Nairobi*, 8.

5. Lefever, *Amsterdam to Nairobi*, 8.

certainty and absoluteness deposited in the belief system also carries a presumption that to be good, someone else must be bad.

One ensuing question that faces us in this inquiry is the authenticity of the story. Whose story is much invested in the his-story of Christian mission? Major texts on the history of Christianity excessively focus on Europe as the epicenter of Christianity. In this narrative, the spread of Christianity began unilaterally from the West to the East or from North to South. Christianity is viewed as a Western religion. That impression seriously hampers the development of Christianity in other parts of the world. It can trigger memories and raise a red flag for new waves of colonial expansion. General knowledge about God, people, and the world is largely authenticated by Western patriarchal values and systems. The authentication of a Western worldview further reinforces genealogical ways of knowledge used for studying people and their cultures.

Knowledge is inevitably attended by power. But when the power fails to lift up insurgent agency or respect valuable critique, that power of knowledge is larger than knowledge *per se*. This form of power cannot be liberating, but domineering. The episteme that highlights the scientific knowledge constitutes a kind of social control subjugating those outside of the power circles. Thus Edward Said contended that knowledge represents thoroughly a kind of power that dominates the discourse of life at all levels.[6] Power over other is more than an opinion, but actively at work in politics, international relations, and economic matters. Even in our everyday life, power takes the form of cultural dominance. Art, music, literature, food, and even language, contain implicit sets of moral values that characterize what civilization is. But those standards can sanction deviance and difference.

In *Transforming Mission*, David Bosch unhesitatingly questioned the conflation of Christian mission with the naïve epistemological triumphalism ingrained in Enlightenment rationality.[7] Bosch realizes that "Our theologies are partial, and they are culturally and socially biased. They may never claim to be absolutes."[8] For Bosch, Western privatization of the missionary movement in Christian history is questionable. While his challenge

6. Said, *Orientalism*, 2–3.

7. Bosch believed Christians of the twentieth century found themselves in the midst of the most important moments in the history of Christian mission. It was a time when Christians expanded their consciousness to the impacts of the Enlightenment. The Enlightenment's overemphasis on reason and rationality distorted the basis and nature of Christian mission. Therefore Bosch asserted that the foundation of mission is not built on human thoughts, but the self-definition of Jesus whose teaching consistently challenges the attitudes of his disciples and their acts of building walls and drawing boundaries between one another. See Bosch, *Transforming Mission*.

8. Bosch, *Transforming Mission*, 190.

against Western domineering desires and rejection of Western worldview and philosophy upon missionary encounter are widely known, Bosch's proposal is limited in various respects. He relied heavily on European and American scholarship. In a sense, his talk of epistemology does not represent a complete break with Western value and tradition. His analysis of the six missionary paradigms only slightly involved the insights and inputs of theologians and missiologists in the South.[9] The paradigm shift may take place among Western missiologists and thinkers alike, but the practice of self-examination intrinsic to the change does not revolutionize the shape and makeup of leadership in the field. Mission agendas are frequently set by Western leadership that decides where the money goes. Far from representing a game-changer in Christian missionary movement, Bosch's proposal of the paradigm shift tends to portray a linear historical development of Christian mission. I do not think Bosch would want to follow the footsteps of the Enlightenment thinkers. He was urgently seeking solutions for the future of Christian mission; however, the core assumptions about the other in missiological exploration remain intact. Marion Grau comments that Bosch's account "proceeds in a familiar missiological frame, exclusively focusing on the missionaries, the societies and theological movements they were embedded in. . . . It is also far from clear that he has addressed the heritage of colonial missions and the inherent thought patterns substantially."[10] Joerg Rieger maintains, "Without having to worry about colonialism and the associated (mis)use of power and authority any more, mission and missionary enterprises now seem to be free to reinvent themselves."[11]

A Quest for Reconstructing Historical Accounts: Promoting the Diversity of Voices

The direction of history is not necessarily headed in a linear way, as Bosch described. It depends on one's critical reading strategy. Historian Philip Jenkins reminds us of the fact that "Christianity was polyglot."[12] Unfortunately some Christian communities in Asia and Africa were not able to survive

9. I am not saying Bosch completely ignored churches in the South with which he actually was much concerned. Bosch might even advocate the diversity of voices in the field of mission studies; however, ideas and theologies of Christian leaders and theologians in the South were not meaningfully engaged in his reconstructed missionary paradigms.

10. Grau, *Rethinking Mission in the Postcolony*, 34.

11. Rieger quoted in Grau, *Rethinking Mission in the Postcolony*, 34.

12. Jenkins, *Lost History of Christianity*, 77.

life-threatening anti-Christian actions hundreds to a thousand years ago. The loss of world Christianity revealed not only how we see history, but also how we label other Christians outside the circle of Europeans. The decline of Christianity in the two mentioned continents was made equivalent to a failure. Since our minds are so conditioned to success, failure in Christian mission became a taboo. As a result, we ignore the people, their existence, and that part of history. Their stories subsequently went unheard. In other words, the perception that history is linear emerges out of the condition in which we have wiped out what has been deemed unsuccessful attempts of Christian expansion. Western Christianity is once again elevated to be the prototype for churches around the world and since then, this particular form of Christianity has crystallized the nature of our memory. That memory in selection could adversely impact the way we perceive non-Christians in those continents that failed to proselytize.

In protest against power hierarchies in world Christianity, Justo Gonzalez challenged the inclination of making Western civilization the norm of Christianity. Gonzalez argued for a new cartography of Christian history. Gonzalez claims,

> If history is a drama, then geography is the stage on which the action flows. . . . It was only when I began seeing them as actual people with their feet on the ground, and when I began understanding the movements of peoples and nations not only across time and chronology but also across space and geography, that history became fascinating to me.[13]

History is about people. It concerns the activity of every kind of people in the land. Putting it simply, the story of humanity is made up of multiple voices and there should be more than one account of the history of Christianity. When we take seriously Acts 1:8 that says, "But you will receive power when the Holy Spirit has come upon you; and you will be my witnesses in Jerusalem, in all Judea and Samaria, and to the ends of the earth," this is a call open for all disciples of Jesus. The idea of a polycentric map lifts up the matter of diversity that further connects people's experiences and feelings with their witnessing to the gospel. Gonzalez thus argued non-Western Christianity is not merely a part of the missionary movement, but a major constituent of church history. Integrating the history of Christian mission with the history of the church will refashion a missiological ecclesiology that further enlarges the vision of inclusivity among God's people.[14]

13. Gonzalez, *Changing Shape of Church History*, 7–8.
14. See Cardoza-Orlandi and Gonzalez, *To All Nations from All Nations*.

The study of Christian mission indeed requires a radical reconstruction of historical events. Both Jenkins and Gonzalez are faithfully advocating the multiplicity of voices that further provides us with a more responsible reading strategy for the history of Christianity.

Nowadays, many have been aware that the center of gravity in global Christianity has shifted to the South. Because of its overwhelming surge of Christian population, churches in the South are given more opportunities to get involved in the discussion of their issues. In terms of numbers and vitality, it is inevitable that the voices of the South need to be heard. Their participation, insights, and wisdom will bridge the epistemological discrepancy that has long existed in the Christian missionary movement. In the meantime, Christian communities are widespread which further convinces us that anywhere across the globe can be a center of attention; for the Spirit of God blows wherever it pleases.[15] The presence of the other forces us to question our identity and sense of vocation in challenging the theology in our times. Our missiology, good or bad, shapes our view of the other, which affects the way we interact with the other. How one treats another human being, under the banner of advancing the gospel is an important subject that needs constant evaluation. There is no question about it.

The Need for a New Approach

The new focus on the Christian missionary movement should take on the intersectionality of power, and the linguistic and theological conceptualization of difference. It requires an interdisciplinary approach to analyze the materialization of binary opposites. I will look at historical rhetoric in Christian mission with the aids of critical theory and linguistic reflection.[16] These disciplines may represent very different approaches, but in this study they are not mutually exclusive. Rather, these divergent insights complement and build upon one another. I purposely argue that the relationship between

15. Cf. John 3:8. One of the recent trends of mission studies is to examine missionary work in a pneumatological framework. As the work of the Holy Spirit sustains life of every form, it becomes a critical point in the history of God's creation and redemption. There is no longer a division between old churches and young churches, Christians and non-Christians; people including those of other faiths are all recipients of God's grace. The mission of the Spirit puts into question the practice of subjugating unchurched and adherents of other religions, marking a significant change in dealing with religious pluralism. See Yong and Clarke, *Global Renewal, Religious Pluralism.*

16. Engaging Christian mission can indeed be done through a variety of views; and as varied perspectives intertwine, it is not unorthodox to utilize an idea which is secular. It will instead turn out an unfinished business if omitting an idea which happens to be secular.

giver and receiver of mission needs to be understood in the framework of self and other. Theories of self and other matter across disciplines, and they can effectively analyze the intersecting interests between one another and give reasons for people's behaviors in the context of social life. The concep- tualization of giver as self and receiver as other is both urgent and relevant. It is because the self-centric approach to Christian mission has confused and kept the giver from recognizing the selfhood of an-other-self, that is, the receiver. Privileging self over other in the form of mission discourses remains problematic. Language will take us back to where we began, that is, the creation and manipulation of otherness for the sake of sustaining Christian mission. It is important to examine how otherness is constructed and interpreted to fit into the paradigm of the Christian missionary movement. I will explain that in more detail.

Self and Other in Mission Discourses

The subject of the other is as old as humanity. Ample literature and resources are available concerning the issue of binarial relations. Edward Said once observed that other was not born to be other, but was made to being the Other.[17] Otherness—including but not limited to ontological and epistemological traits of the other—is turned into a point of reference for people inside power circles to deal with those outside of it.[18] In the discipline of philosophy, Martin Buber's *I-Thou* concept is helpful for us to reflect on the very subject of inter-personal relationships. Buber declared that words are not things, but relationships. Buber says, "When a primary word is spoken the speaker enters the word and takes his stand in it."[19] The primary word, Buber considers, *I-Thou* later became an influential concept for the relation of things. Seeing another person as my *Thou* would avoid reducing a human being to an *It*.[20] Since I and You (or other) share the most basic humanity, "we" are equally entitled to life and dignity without discrimination. On the one hand, Buber's observation confronts head-on the objectification of people; on the other hand, Buber emphasizes the importance of mutual respect for the sake of building healthy relationships. His idea discreetly works to alter the way we deal with human beings who are different from us.

17. Said, *Orientalism*, 5–6.

18. Said, *Orientalism*, 2.

19. Buber, *I and Thou*, 19–20.

20. Buber, *I and Thou*, 23–24.

Man speaks in many tongues—tongues of language, of art, of action—but the spirit is one. . . . In truth language does not reside in man but man stands in language and speaks out of it—so it is with all words, all spirit. . . . Spirit is not in the I but between I and You. It is not like the blood that circulates in you but like the air in which you breathe. Man lives in the spirit when he is able to respond to his You. He is able to do that when he enters into this relation with his whole being.[21]

There are however questions to ask. If "relation is mutual"[22] in its fundamental nature as Buber argues, how does encountering other civilizations in the so-called mission fields easily result in putting people into categories? The giver-receiver relation has proved to be an antithesis of the *I-Thou* concept. We form unity by giving the receiver a label of "other." We form barriers between us and them, which allow us to claim that we are good and they are bad. These barriers are human constructs. While Buber's *I-Thou* concept offers rich analytical possibilities of understanding human relationships, the binary between giver and receiver in the context of Christian mission persists. Why is the ideal form of relationships, as *I-Thou*, not realized to its fullest? What obstructs the disposition of *I-Thou* relation from happening thoroughly? I do not completely rule out Buber's observation, for precisely Buber points out that self is where I am speaking from; a self-centric vantage point easily subjugates another I as an object. Buber's argument in human relations is valuable, but it does not always guarantee mutuality in direct relationship with others. It does not specifically explain to us how we communicate with the other through our daily social interactions. The operations of Christian mission are far more complex than that. The problem of relational disorder in Christian mission exposes deeper issues in epistemological principles, theological orientation and praxis. We need more than metaphysical knowledge to address the ontological problem present in the civilizing mission.

It is time to stop avoiding the elephant in the room; it is time to address the recurring problem of power differential in the Christian missionary movement. That power, embodied in the form of discourses, easily distorted and falsified the value of other cultures and religions. The examination of how mission discourses function is the order of the day, in particular, how that accelerates the prioritization of the negative in binary opposites used for evangelistic purposes. The number of publications with the term "mission discourses" included in their titles is getting more accessible; however,

21. Buber, *I and Thou*, 88–89.
22. Buber, *I and Thou*, 23.

the work that analyses—implicitly and explicitly—relations between mission discourses and the construction of otherness is scattered. In reviewing literature that focuses on the link between language and missionary work, Esme Cleall's analysis of the discourse of difference is particularly useful. In *Missionary Discourses of Difference*, Cleall asserts that "difference" is an essential component in any mission discourse. The concept of difference, as Cleall explains, is "the practice of making 'like' from 'unlike,' a way of positioning things, people and concepts relationality."[23] Putting it in another way, the sustainability of the mission enterprise depends very much on how difference is articulated.

After examining missionary writings of the London Missionary Society (LMS), Cleall argues that "difference" was utilized to construct binary oppositions. For instance, the British Empire was associated with light whereas the rest of the world dark.[24] The portrayal of opposing images not only necessitates the Empire's civilizing mission, but also consolidates the creation of self-identity.[25] Cleall also provided convincing evidence of the connection between the concept of difference and mission discourses by contesting the legitimization of colonial thinking in missionary activities peculiarly in the areas of home-making, sickness and racialization within the "heathen" land. Her work seriously challenges conventional mission studies that have shown an inclination to self-glorify past achievements.

Similar to Cleall's research focus, Webb Keane questions the epistemological privilege of the church over human value. Keane's critique of missionary activity as a form of cultural aggression has taken a new twist on the subject of Christian mission. The entire Christian missionary movement is contingent on "certain semiotic forms and ideologies." In traversing the perimeter of missionary encounters, Keane observes that

> The globalization of Protestant Christianity was facilitated by the development of certain semiotic forms and ideologies. Some of these have become inseparable from even the purportedly secular narratives of modernity. . . . The particular forms taken by colonialism's long-term influence in many parts of the post-colonial world are surely marked, in some way, by missionaries' moral impetus to improve the world.[26]

23. Cleall, *Missionary Discourses of Difference*, 3.

24. Cleall, *Missionary Discourses of Difference*, 2.

25. Cleall, *Missionary Discourses of Difference*, 2.

26. With his experience in postcolonial Indonesia, Webb Keane examined the issue of agency in missionary encounter. He is concerned with the way people receive words and things that have been spoken and presented to them. Keane, *Christian Moderns*, 42–43.

✳ Language is not innocent. The way that specific language is used, a statement made and a story told is all calculated and manipulated. The categories of modern/backward, cultured/barbaric, and so forth are implicated and constructed for the production of cultural representations that further condones binary oppositions against the other.

Unlike Cleall, Keane pointed out the narrative of modernity has influenced the life of both converts and nonconverts. As soon as the converts inherit the legacy of the missionary culture, they will pass on the imported cultural practice to his or her own people.[27] Keane insisted that new problems in the local church probably resulted from "the same fundamental problems."[28] More significantly, Keane's observation has affirmed that identity is fluid. Because of its fluidity, identity is not singular. Under the canopy of hybridized identities, local converts could turn out to assume the role of the former missionary. Indeed over the last hundred years, Christianity has experienced variations and reversals in its demographics. Everyone is overjoyed with the profound shift of the gravity of Christianity to the South. But no one would want to see churches in the South "repeat" the missionary practice of the West in the "heathen land." The word "repeat" suggests a continuation of unchecked mission discourses used for problematizing otherness, recruiting missionaries, securing funds and other related missionary activities. The same old strategy of condemning people other than Christian is unfortunately prevalent and it actually undergirds the mission agenda of many churches in East Asia. The weight of misrepresentation of the other takes place upon missionary encounter. Christians set up boundaries against non-Christians. The us versus them is not just a truism, but an ideology that excludes.

The Christian Missionary Movement as a Constructed Discourse

Discourses on the mission of God have been constantly misused to do harm to the other time and again. From the crusaders' intolerance "in the name of God" to heathen conversion "for the kingdom of God," the longstanding hostility to the other or simply xenophobia has not been removed from public discourses on the other. There is every reason to believe that the entire Christian missionary movement is something other than a sheer venture of holiness. The kind of violence done to non-Christians and people of different religious traditions not only exposes a problematic reading of the mission of God, but also creates a "reality" justifying the continual subjugation

27. Keane, *Christian Moderns*, 9.
28. Keane, *Christian Moderns*, 9.

of the other. The reality of Christian mission is evidently operating within the framework of social construction.

The idea of a socially constructed reality is not new. Since the 1960s, Peter Berger and Thomas Luckmann have broadened the scope of sociology of religion by connecting knowledge with reality. In their propositions, human knowledge comes into existence from the interactions with social conditions. The knowledge inherited from that will construct what has been known as our "reality." Berger and Luckmann claim, "Society is a human product. Society is an objective reality."[29] The social reality is internalized into ourselves through human activity, and the externalized human activity becomes objective that makes the reality independent from us yet allows us to share that with other individuals.[30] The idea of the socially constructed reality can help us understand the operation of religion. Says Berger,

> Religion is the human enterprise by which a sacred cosmos is established. . . . It can be said that religion has played a strategic part in the human enterprise of world-building. Religion implies the farthest reach of man's self-externalization, of his infusion of reality with his own meanings. Religion implies that human order is projected into the totality of being. Put differently religion is the audacious attempt to conceive of the entire universe as being humanly significant.[31]

The procedures of social control are deposited into the character of reality, including the religious one. While maintaining the order of things, the process of identity-formation takes place in these socially constructed worlds.

With regard to how meaning is derived in and communicated in the socially constructed reality, I will turn to John R. Searle's idea of social reality. In his important work titled *The Construction of Social Reality*, Searle claimed that social behaviors have always been understood in collective terms. The act of collective behaviors reflects the kind of collective intentionality that "is essential to understanding social facts."[32] Social facts are also known as institutional facts that represent "a structure of power relations, including negative and positive, conditional and categorical, collective and individual powers."[33] These powers can create meaning for members of the community in their daily living, regulate relations between members of

29. Berger and Luckmann, *Social Construction of Reality*, 61.

30. Berger and Luckmann, *Social Construction of Reality*, 59–61.

31. Berger, *Sacred Canopy*, 25–28.

32. Searle, *Construction of Social Reality*, 23–24.

33. Searle, *Construction of Social Reality*, 94.

the community through an imposition of rights and obligations, and help members to achieve higher social status.[34] However when collective intentionality is driven by biased vision and selfish purposes, collective social behaviors can be destructive, which further approves a lopsided reality to maintain the consensus of the mass.

Growing out of Searle's concept of a socially constructed reality, otherness is created through the daily operation of Christian mission in order to serve the interests of relevant mission agencies and societies. The construction of otherness functions as a projection of thought by self. What one thinks about the other will immediately be translated to the public. Is that perception of others trustworthy? For Michael A. Rynkiewich, missionary account indicates a tendency to speak incorrectly of the other. After exploring the boundaries between self, mind and society, Rynkiewich concludes that Christians tend to "make sense of a reality that comes to us in fragments."[35]

Language is not neutral. Our biased opinions about the other can be vicious. When a socially constructed self mistakenly receives and re-formulates prejudicial perspectives about the other, related missionary practice that demonizes other cultures and religions will continually be a norm. Therefore, understanding the construction of social reality is inseparable from analyzing the power of discourses. According to Michel Foucault, the objectivity of truth depends on the discourse of truth.[36] Foucault questions the mechanism that governs a statement and the validation of it.[37] More than being attentive to the syntax and semantics of a statement, Foucault challenges the way knowledge is formed. Foucault warns us to be careful of the relations between discourses and truth. Truth expresses itself in the form of knowledge that we agreed on. Knowledge immediately shapes social behaviors and relations operated in politics, international relations, and even the expansion of Christianity. Furthermore, the close connection between discourses and self/other binary are not one-way. They work both ways. While mission discourses intensify the self/other binary, the latter authorizes the value of the former. The happening of self versus other testifies to the fact that a power differential has evolved out of the existing relations between two parties. The interaction of the two parties expresses itself in the form of a binary. The vicious cycle of a power differential entrapped in

34. Searle, *Construction of Social Reality*, 94–102.

35. Rynkiewich, *Soul, Self, and Society*, 14.

36. Foucault, *Power/Knowledge*, 119.

37. The major concern for Foucault is not about scientific validity or a scientific approach to knowledge but the way a statement of truth is made. Foucault, *Power/Knowledge*, 112–13.

the mission discourses can intensify mistrust and unequal treatment of the other even in the context of mission partnership.

Discourses can shape human subjectivity. The subjectivity of each individual is to be recognized, and the fact that each individual is a subject by nature should compel Christians across traditions to take seriously the larger question about agency in missionary encounters. Attaining full personhood of the other is undoubtedly an indispensable part of Christian mission. If missionary activities are creative expressions of God's grace upon all forms of life, acknowledging the diversity of voices will eventually be beneficial for a new praxis of mission to emerge.

Organization of This Book

Chapter 2 provides some basic linguistic theories to help us understand what language is and how it functions. Language is not simply about conveying people's thoughts. According to John R. Searle, language has the capacity to create a reality that obliges people to act and speak in a certain way. The aspect that language can shape our perception of the world becomes essential for the evaluation of the close connection between language and otherness in the history of Christianity. This new role of language leads us to re-evaluate George Lindbeck's cultural-linguistic model, which has been influential in shaping theological, biblical, and missiological discussion. Lindbeck might have successfully created a reality that is mediated through language, but the reality of Christianity becomes totally dependent on the overarching theme of salvation. When the reality is dominated by this metanarrative, Christians rely on this reality to give them meaning. But unfortunately, it is also that reality that differentiates Christians from non-Christians. The rigidity of the Christian identity can cause a wide range of problems for missionary endeavors. The metanarrative itself does not pose a problem, but it is the group of people that uses the exclusive speech to problematize the other community. Power differentials between the narrator and the narrated create a self/other binary that could drastically affect the well-being of the other.

Chapter 3 identifies the discourses used for missionary endeavors in relation to categorization and misrepresentation of the other. The analysis is based largely on mission literature and publications, including William Carey's *Enquiry*, reports on the World Missionary Conference in Edinburgh (1910), The WCC's *Guidelines on Dialogue with People of Living Faiths and Ideologies*, The Vatican's *Ad Gentes* and *Nostra Aetate*, and other modern mission documents. To revisit past mission discourses is not to reinforce past achievements. Rather, it is a sincere reflection on the past that shall prompt one to admit the mistakes and harm done to others in the name of Christian mission. Notice that mission discourses do change over time. The changing patterns of mission discourses are natural responses to the materiality of life. The process of decolonization particularly in the second half of the twentieth century resulted in an increase of self-awareness among the formerly colonized subjects. Churches in the South also started to question the power and knowledge deposited in the civilizing mission. Contesting an imposed order means to say no to coercive evangelism and to say yes to establishing self-identities in the currents of linguistic violence.

Chapter 4 rethinks the notion of self understood in the Christian missionary movement. A self-centric approach to mission primarily resulted from a culture that breeds individualism. The individualistic understanding of self is unfortunately devoid of a communal sense. Self neither carries a connotation of a "we" nor functions as a community of selves. Self refers to an "I" that forms a boundary and separates "I" from my neighbor. When missionary work marginalizes the voice of others, good works become a camouflage for promoting narcissistic values. To confront self-centric intentions, Jesus' self-emptying acts in Philippians 2:1–11 is particularly relevant. The use of biblical resource highlights the importance of humility while engaging missionary work. Emmanuel Levinas's notion of alterity, juxtaposed with the Confucian concept of *ren* (humanity) meanwhile reiterates the inseparability of self and other. The encounter of the other *per se* instinctively connects and carries ethical obligations. The interrelatedness of self and other should lead to a whole new level of human solidarity by enlightening us to take responsibility for the well-being of the other. The renewed sense of self compels one to work with the other face-to-face that helps shatter the binary of us and them. Fostering intercultural relationships will usher in a new direction for missiological exploration.

The new vision for missionary movement is immediately followed by a recovery of self-identities of others. Chapter 5 attempts to reevaluate the whole idea of otherness. It first deconstructs established discourses on the other. Humanization in missionary work tends to focus on livelihood improvement. Full personhood of the other is not seriously engaged. The issue of agency comes to be decisive for missiological exploration if the mission enterprise must deliver value to all stakeholders in its undertakings. A more direct and effective way of upholding the dignity of other is to see otherness as gift. This affirmation does not aim to essentialize the other, but represents an incredible game-changer in the entire enterprise. Examples of encountering the poor and the Hindu will demonstrate the intelligibility of other forms of religious language and practice. The discourse of otherness as gift means that these people do not passively receive information from their senses; rather they actively construct ideas and generate meaning from what they hear and interpret inputs on the basis of existing ideas and previous experience. The voice of others means more than a symbolic token, but a living wisdom that turns the table of missiological agenda, discussion, and practice. The discourse of otherness as gift can further subvert the narrative world of missioner, and consequently, the imbalance of power in the Christian missionary movement. This subversive discourse unmasks the ideology of hegemony that aims to dominate decision-making process and eventually erase otherness.

The concluding chapter calls for a new language that can guard against aggressive use of language to objectify and subjugate others in the name of Christian mission. If language is related to the construction of otherness, language should be able to help us cross the boundaries that shut people out. Any shift in language should be motivated, undergirded, and sustained by God's reconciling work. Missiological language can thus facilitate mutuality and build up an ongoing dialogue with the other. Finally, the new language will enable us to expand our language of God through diverse and divergent expressions of witnesses. Knowledge is not a closed system. When we envision God exclusively through analogies and imaginaries within a specific culture or group of people, we end up limiting God to certain imageries. Learning to relate to different groups of people and be empathetic to their struggles and aspirations further guide us to God's wondrous work done among people across cultures and languages.

This book extends an invitation for churches and Christians to make space for the other. Together we can develop a new language that aims to build trust and foster relationship in missionary encounter. In radicalizing otherness, this book hopes to open new avenues to witnessing to God's unfailing love to all people, regardless of difference. Because of that love, we can love others as ourselves.

2

Language and Otherness

WHAT IS LANGUAGE? WHAT does language do? This chapter will first unveil bias in language. I will approach linguistic theory through the humanities and social sciences. Basic concepts of linguistics allow us to see how language is associated with social behaviors. These concepts will further raise our awareness of the connection between language and otherness. Then we may ask: Whose language do we speak in Christian mission? This important question will help us explore the role of language in the expansion of Christianity.

Debunking the Myth of Linguistic Neutrality

Those who consider language purely a medium to communicate meanings are inclined to think language is neutral. Since the neutrality of language is recurrently asserted rather than argued, people find it convenient to apply uncritically the principle of linguistic neutrality to the study of Christian mission. Before analyzing the relation between language and otherness, it is necessary to point out that language can be problematic. Below are some simple examples of what biased language can do.

Bias in Language

Stories related to declining worship attendance are capturing the headlines in recent days. It is not my area of focus to explore whether or not the church is shrinking in the United States. I am more concerned with how the story is narrated and what implications are there for the readers. One popular phenomenon people are talking about is that "Christianity is dying." This statement provides a good starting point for describing the problem of whose Christianity we are referring to in a pluralistic society such as the United States of America. That "Christianity is dying" largely describes the rapid decrease of members in white mainline congregations and the shrinking also presents a threat to their pride and privilege. The vitality of ethnic Christian communities in America however proves the opposite. Congregations of Spanish-speaking, Korean-speaking, Chinese-speaking and the like are thriving. Whose language are "we" supposed to speak in this specific context?

To the comfort of many souls, spirituality is simply "shifting" and as missiologists and historians have projected decades ago, the gravitational center of Christianity has shifted to the South. But even the discourse of "Christianity is moving from Global North to Global South" is insufficient to describe the complexity of the development of Christian history. The North to South discourse inadvertently left the East unattended.[1] According to Dyron B. Daughrity,

> Christianity begins in the Middle East, dis-seminates across the Mediterranean region through missionary endeavors, rises to imperial status during the reign of Constantine, slowly but surely recedes from "the East" and becomes something much more characterized as a Western European phenomenon, migrates across the Atlantic during the age of exploration, almost vanishes from Western Europe, and reinvents itself in the "Global South," or, Asia, Africa, and Latin America. Many of us inherited this narrative of Christian history.[2]

The retelling of the story of Christianity showed how Daughrity reacted to cultural and missional insensitivity to *other* Christian communities across the world. In line with Philip Jenkins and Justo Gonzalez and others, Daughrity spoke against the misrepresentation of world Christianity and questioned the Eurocentric thinking undergirding the entire movement. The emerging concept of a geographical shift of the center of Christianity from North to South strengthens the traditional cartography of missionary activities. It means that the typical narrative of Christian history entirely ignored 'the East.' By the East, Daughrity referred to the Orthodox Church. Eradicating the Christian communities of the East from the history of Christianity is an act of betrayal. Daughrity unremittingly points out, "Orthodox Christianity is ancient and has survived against the odds. Orthodox Christians see themselves as having preserved a precious treasure by maintaining

---

1. Dyron B. Daughrity, "Ignoring the East: Correcting a Serious Flaw in World Christianity Scholarship," in Adogame and Shankar, *Religion on the Move!*, 42–46.

2. Daughrity, "Ignoring the East," 43.

their teachings and traditions."[3] Any ideas that suggest otherwise only reinforce the existing narrative. Its embedded triumphalism is further enforced by layers of languages. This explains why Daughrity considers "the new 'North to South' story of Christian expansion . . . a continuation of the old Western narrative of Christian development."[4]

The Hegemony of English in Christian Mission

The two examples above can well illustrate how English wording dominates the discussion of Christian history. As a matter of fact, the rise of English did not appear suddenly. The English language has been strategized as a tool to conquer, civilize, and proselytize. In Gary McGee's analysis of language preparation for missionary work, he writes,

> In the latter part of the century, as European colonial empires began to reach their farthest extent, American imperialism flourished and acquired its greatest gains as a result of the Spanish-American War of 1898. Anglo-Saxons on both sides of the Atlantic looked forward to the days when the English language would become the international means of communication. With more than a whiff of Social Darwinism, Josiah Strong, general secretary of the Evangelical Alliance of the United States, announced that the English language "is better fitted than any other to become, and . . . is actually becoming more and more, a world-language."[5]

Josiah Strong's statement was originally published in *The New Era: Or, the Coming Kingdom* in 1893. English evolved into a global language in the twenty-first century.[6] Some may think that Strong's prophesy made more than a hundred and twenty years ago has finally come true. One thing is certain: Teaching English abroad becomes an effective mission strategy that accelerates the dominant role of the language. Teaching English to

3. Daughrity, "Ignoring the East," 42.

4. Daughrity, "Ignoring the East," 46.

5. Gary McGee criticized those who urged to evangelize the world for not being interested in learning the indigenous languages. Their prayer for the gift of tongues in order to preach the gospel to the unsaved only buttressed the superior position of their own language. McGee, "Shortcut to Language Preparation?," 118.

6. BBC News ran an article titled "How English Evolved into a Global Language." While giving reason for the need of an international language, the article highlights the legacy of the British Empire. It claims, "Benefitting from the legacy of the British Empire, and the rise in influence of the most powerful member of that Empire—the USA—English (or kinds of English) is being spoken all over the globe."

"non-native speakers" not only offers an opportunity for Christians to connect with those who have never heard about the gospel, but also provides a "legitimate" way for missionaries to enter countries which legally prohibit religious workers.

This research study does not investigate why English becomes a global language, but interrogates how language impacts Christian missionary activities and their relations with the missionized. Felix Ehimare Enegho and Friday John Imekh, who are concerned with the marginalization of their native language, Nigerian Pidgin English, critique,

> Most missionaries who came to Africa spoke their own languages and were quite comfortable with the assistance of local interpreters to put their message across to their audience, even when they were not sure if the right message was transmitted to their hearers. Most of these missionaries, practically out of desperation, forced their audience to speak their own Western language through the introduction of schools. Though such schools were for the purpose of making the people literate through a Western education, most missionaries for their own part were not interested in learning the language of the people; since as far as the missionaries were concerned, the local languages were difficult to learn and not relevant to their mission.[7]

Missionaries can certainly tell the challenge of learning another language, but the feeling is mutual. Enticing the indigenous people to speak the language of missionaries in the name of promoting a single international language is already doubtful. Failing to see value in the language(s) of the people fails one to see and appreciate biblical understandings of diversity. Missionary activities become even more suspicious with the entanglement of problematic theological orientation, limited vision statements, and discriminatory practice. Thus Enegho and Imekh assert, "Even today, language is often a significant obstacle to the hearing and understanding of the gospel. At times, the institutional church insists on the proclamation of the good news in a language that is foreign and unknown to the hearers. This is a direct and deliberate contradiction of the spirit of Pentecost."[8]

There are indeed hundreds of thousands of languages spoken in respective cultural contexts, which is a fact that no one can deny. In reality, we find ourselves in an awkward situation when Bengali, Hindi, Mandarin Chinese are mostly and widely spoken throughout the world, yet it is English that becomes dominant in many occasions including politics and international

7. Enegho and Imaekhai, "Language and Christian Evangelism," 340.

8. Enegho and Imaekhai, "Language and Christian Evangelism," 339–40.

relations. In a similar vein, Euro-English languages are represented in international missiological conferences. Ironically, speakers of non-Western languages are re-presented by Euro-English based mission agencies, and furthermore, mission literature written in "indigenous" languages is largely considered unmarketable by publishing houses in Western societies.[9]

No language is devoid of human assumptions. The urge for responsible and appropriate language is precisely saying no to the hegemonic rhetoric that rallies for a specific gender, race, theology, and missionary practice. When missiologists, historians, and church leaders are unwilling to admit that the neutrality in language is a myth, the discourse of Christian mission continues to run along the framework of narrating the achievements of missionary work with excessive pride.

What Is Language?

Language matters. The choice of word is not random. Words and sentences can be expressions of power and identity. The use of a specific word never carries neutral meaning; rather, it bears cultural values and attitudes that directly condition our social relationships. How one's language can enjoy the position of privilege and advantage over other languages in the world is not a coincidence. Linguists Laurie Bauer and Peter Trudgill observe that "the superiority of one language or dialect over another [has] social and historical rather than genuinely linguistic origins." This speaks clearly that not all languages receive equal status. Bauer and Trudgill go on to say that "languages and dialects are unique and miraculous products of the human brain and human society."[10] Therefore, the study of language will have to

---

9. In a workshop discussing the publishing trends in the field of missiology, organized by the American Society of Missiology in 2015, spokespersons and editors of major Christian publishers indicated that they had a tendency to invite and approve proposals drafted only by scholars of color who are widely known. The primary reason is that their projects and literature are more marketable than those who are lesser known. Respective publishers will not publish work that does not guarantee profits. While publishers are not willing to take the risk of approving proposals by budding scholars, many of them simply remain an underdog. Since their work never gets published, they rarely receive attention. Their work will not be marketable, because they remain lesser known to the public. The vicious cycle explains itself. The not-getting-published or not-marketable conundrum further encourages professors and instructors of mission classes to recommend to students the texts and materials written primarily by native English-speakers. Chances are students will receive less exposure to the diversity of cultural perspectives.

10. Bauer and Trudgill, *Language Myths*.

take into consideration the overall structures of society, including the interactions between one another and the implications on social behaviors.

Ferdinand de Saussure: The Arbitrariness of Language

On defining language, Ferdinand de Saussure, a pioneer in developing the discipline of structural linguistics into a branch of broader science, asserted that language (*langue*) is not some random spoken words which are independent of one another. Language (*langue*) and speaking (*parole*) makes the speech (*langage*). According to Saussure, language is "both a social product of the faculty of speech and a collection of necessary conventions that have been adopted by a social body to permit individuals to exercise that faculty."[11] Language, in short, "is a system of signs that express ideas."[12] Thought and sound are originally two "shapeless masses" and language connects these two masses into an ordered entity.[13] Saussure called the combination of thought and sound "a form" and a form is not identical with "a substance."[14] It works the way similar to a sign that does not mean what the thing really *is* but what the thing refers to. Thus a form is also understood as a "linguistic sign" that unites a sound and a concept.[15] Each sign consists of the signifier (a sound) and the signified (the idea which the signifier expresses). The relationship between the two is called signification. For instance, a tree is pronounced as "tree" (signifier) and meanwhile, bears the concept of a tree (signified). Each linguistic sign contains phonic and psychological elements (where the latter concerns senses and thoughts). The combination of both elements appears to make each linguistic sign "independent and self-contained."[16] But this is not true. The nature of language has to be understood in relation to other semiological systems. This structural emphasis is what makes Saussure a founder of structuralism.

Saussure did not answer questions such as, why is a tree called "tree" and where does the concept of a tree come from? Instead, he was interested in the arbitrary nature of the linguistic sign.[17] "The bond between the signifier and the signified is arbitrary," Saussure emphasized.[18] Since a word has

11. Saussure, *Course in General Linguistics*, 9.

12. Saussure, *Course in General Linguistics*, 16.

13. Saussure, *Course in General Linguistics*, 112.

14. Saussure, *Course in General Linguistics*,113.

15. Saussure, *Course in General Linguistics*, 66.

16. Saussure, *Course in General Linguistics*, 114.

17. Saussure, *Course in General Linguistics*, 113.

18. Saussure, *Course in General Linguistics*, 67.

no meaning intrinsically, giving an idea to a thing through uttering a sound is arbitrary. Though a linguistic sign is more than a naming-process, naming the thing itself is actually an act of "arbitrariness."[19] Saussure says,

> The arbitrary nature of the sign explains in turn why the so-cial fact alone can create a linguistic system. The community is necessary if values that owe their existence solely to usage and general acceptance are to be set up; by himself the individual is incapable of fixing a single value.[20]

For Saussure, the arbitrariness of a linguistic sign does not mean "That is just the way it is." Saussure instead believed the arbitrary nature of the sign became the rule that effectively assists linguists to understand what meaning the people are trying to convey. Linguistics therefore becomes a kind of science that deals with an impersonal system of signs. Thus he says, "The task of the linguist is to find out what makes language a special system within the mass of semiological data."[21] It was how respective linguistic systems work within a specific community that caught Saussure's attention, but not an individual's use of language and the effect of the subsequent linguistic implications on others. When the whole community takes seriously the arbitrary sign, the signs become a system for meaning-making. The signs bring to light the reality underneath respective cultural expressions.

Saussure sees language as "a self-contained whole" that enables people to communicate and share memories with one another in a given culture or locality. More importantly, language provides "a principle of classification."[22] Saussure argues that "in language there are only differences. . . . Whether we take the signified or the signifier, language has neither ideas nor sounds that existed before the linguistic system, but only conceptual and phonic differences that have issued from the system."[23] The idea of classification comes in, not simply because classification is a characteristic of differentiating one thing from another, but it has to do with the value of that specific linguistic system. Here, we touch on an essential element of Saussure's theory which is the linguistic value. We will want to pay attention to that, with respect to its implication for the history of the missionary movement. Saussure claims,

> A linguistic system is a series of differences of sound combined with a series of differences of ideas; but the pairing of a certain

19. Saussure, *Course in General Linguistics*, 113.

20. Saussure, *Course in General Linguistics*, 113.

21. Saussure, *Course in General Linguistics*, 16.

22. Saussure, *Course in General Linguistics*, 9.

23. Saussure, *Course in General Linguistics*, 120.

number of acoustical signs with as many cuts made from the mass of thought engenders a system of values. . . . In language, as in any semiological system, whatever distinguishes one sign from the others constitutes it. Difference makes character just as it makes value and the unit.[24]

Linguistic value cannot be confused with signification.[25] Each linguistic system works out its way for signification, and its linguistic value in a specific cultural context differs from another. Take for example *mouton* in French which may have the same signification as *sheep* in English, but they do not share the same value. The difference in value can best be seen when referencing to the cooked meat. In English, it is called *mutton* and not sheep, whereas, there is no distinction in French.[26] Saussure advanced his argument by citing an example of grammatical rule. He explains,

The value of a French plural does not coincide with that of a Sanskrit plural even though their signification is usually identical; Sanskrit has three numbers instead of two (*my eyes, my ears, my arms, my legs,* etc. are dual); it would be wrong to attribute the same value to the plural in Sanskrit and in French; its value clearly depends on what is outside and around it.

Since no words stand for "pre-existing concepts," there is no standardization for the signifier and signified in linguistic signs across cultures or semiological data in general.[27] The reality that linguistic value varies from one culture to another is legitimate. If difference is necessary, comparing which linguistic system has the best value is meaningless. Difference in value points to one thing: the intelligibility of each linguistic system that includes how that system works and how its value makes sense within a community of people. In Saussure's word, "values remain entirely relative."[28]

Saussure's approach to language became influential, impacting not just linguistics, but also other disciplines, such as anthropology. Building on Saussure's structural linguistics, Claude Levi-Strauss challenged the notion of "primitive" culture. In *The Savage Mind*, Levi-Strauss said people remain entrenched in thought that using abstract words is prevalent among primitive societies, and words such as "abstract," "primitive" are associated with less intelligent and less capable. People fail to recognize that abstractness

---

24. Saussure, *Course in General Linguistics*, 120–21.

25. Saussure, *Course in General Linguistics*, 116.

26. Saussure, *Course in General Linguistics*, 116.

27. Saussure, *Course in General Linguistics*, 116.

28. Saussure, *Course in General Linguistics*, 113.

also exists in the so-called "civilized" languages.[29] It was the feeling of "deficiencies of vocabulary" that has propelled the West to set on its quest for "objective knowledge."[30] Classification is done within the realm of meeting "intellectual requirements rather than or instead of satisfying needs."[31] Levi-Strauss states clearly that "the use of more or less abstract terms is a function not of greater or lesser intellectual capacity, but of differences in the interests—in their intensity and attention to detail—of particular social groups within the national society."[32] While Levi-Strauss did criticize those who belittled people and cultures, his main focus was on classification. Classification reflects the underlying patterns of human thought or the way people understand the world. Like Saussure, Levi-Strauss came to conclude that classification relates to a matter of value which remains relative; meanwhile, classification creates the means of structure dominated by "a pair of contrasts: between general and particular on the one hand, and nature and culture on the other."[33]

Saussure's linguistic theories and Levi-Strauss's cultural concepts may help us understand how one system varies from another linguistically. The existential differences apply to the cultural aspect and worldview of respective communities. They also ask us to withhold our judgment, and to learn to appreciate the underlying meaning involved in human thought as expressed through linguistic signs and cultural acts. However, Saussure's theories did not go without its critics in modern linguistics. While striving for a scientific study of linguistics and the analysis of the objectivity in language, Saussure's theories did not address binary oppositions that exist and are operating within respective cultures. Perhaps, we should come back to Saussure's belief that the perception that whether a given cultural system is good or bad are relative and no one should take the position to judge other cultural-linguistic systems. I do not mean both Saussure and Levi-Strauss endorse "anything goes," but it would be helpful if they could defend their theories from falling prey to relativism. Discussing the plausibility of relativism is beyond the scope of my research; I am more concerned with the implied neutrality of language in the theories. When the world continues to divide along—and even intensify the division of—geographical, religious, and racial lines, is it still reasonable to ignore the inherent power differential between the one who names and the one being named? Michael Oppenheim

29. Levi-Strauss, *Savage Mind*, 1.

30. Levi-Strauss, *Savage Mind*, 1–2.

31. Levi-Strauss, *Savage Mind*, 9.

32. Levi-Strauss, *Savage Mind*, 2.

33. Levi-Strauss, *Savage Mind*, 135.

criticizes, "Ferdinand de Saussure's famous discussion of language as *langue* and *parole*, that is, as system and performance, fails to capture its sensory, affective, formative, dialogical, ethical, and even metaphysical dimensions, which come to the fore in human relationships."[34]

Ample examples indicate the (mis)use of language, including citing the bible for governing purposes. Among them, antisemitism in Nazi ideology and racism during the Apartheid history have already scandalized the religion of Christianity and church history. Propaganda techniques take place primarily through language both written and spoken. If power and language are not addressed properly, chances are that one language will trump all the others. Linguists do not shy away from calling this "linguistic hegemony." Debra Saurez points out, "Linguistic hegemony can be perceived where linguistic minorities will believe in and participate in the subjugation of the minority language to the dominant, to the point where just the dominant language remains."[35]

Again in *Decolonising the Mind*, Ngugi wa Thiong'o believed the introduction of the master's language is a step to remove the people's cultural heritage and eventually their self-identity. Thus Thiong'o observes,

> The effect of a cultural bomb is to annihilate a people's belief in their names, in their languages, in their environment, in their heritage of the struggle, in their unity, in their capacities and ultimately in themselves. It makes them see their past as one wasteland of non-achievement and it makes them want to distance themselves from that wasteland. It makes them want to identify with that which is furthest removed from themselves; for instance, with other peoples' languages rather than their own.[36]

Not only socio-cultural and politico-economic aspects of life, but the spiritual level of humanity can also be affected by the dominant language. George Tinker elucidates how the "colonization of language" limits theological imagination of the divine and reduces that to a male-gendered form fulfilling only the need of a male-centric culture. He sorrowfully says,

> American Indian experiences of the "sacred" (?) Other ("god"?) were almost invariably a bi-gender, reciprocal duality of male and female. Colonization of language, however, has meant that even traditional speakers when speaking in the colonial language (english) will customarily reference the bi-gender

34. Oppenheim, "*Langue, Parole, et Chanson*," 403–4.

35. Suarez, "Paradox of Linguistic Hegemony," 514.

36. Thiong'o, *Decolonising the Mind*, 3.

wako'da with male pronouns, "he," "his," and "him," although they would never do this in their native language.[37]

The imposition of one's cultural value through linguistic means can seriously affect the task of theological construction and missiological orientation. Strictly speaking, the intermingling of language and hegemonic power creates unprecedented consequences to the life of the disadvantaged.

Thus Noam Chomsky considers Saussure's conception of language "impoverished and thoroughly inadequate."[38] Language is much more than a system of its own; Chomsky believes the study of linguistics cannot be separated from "the study of mind and of behavior in general."[39] The point is not to see if language conveys objective meaning, but how the aspect of mental capacities plays into the subject of language. Chomsky says, "Human language can be used to inform or mislead, to clarify one's own thoughts or to display one's cleverness, or simply for play."[40]

On the one hand, we can be sure that the phenomenon of social norms is explainable. According to William Downes, "human minds have an evolved set of cognitive capacities that internalize attitudes of permission or obligation toward contents by virtue of which they become norms."[41] These norms are immediately acted out through language expressions to maintain social order and control. On the other hand, semantics becomes a crucial aspect of linguistics and it is highly context-dependent. The meaning of a sentence has to be placed within its historical and contextual specificities. Context makes a difference. As Homi Bhabha says, there are things that really matter in language, such as, "discursive embeddedness and address, its cultural positionality, its reference to a present time and a specific space."[42] The use of language takes place in concrete spatial, temporal and cultural situations, so that language or the linguistic signs can persuade, coerce, and eventually work in one's favor. Understanding language requires us to take seriously the importance of contextual situations in connection with socialization and its implied social behaviors.

---

37. Tinker, *American Indian Liberation*, 18.

38. Chomsky, *Language and Mind*, 18.

39. Chomsky, *Language and Mind*, 8.

40. Chomsky, *Language and Mind*, 61.

41. Downes, *Language and Religion*, 28

42. Homi K. Bhabha, "Cultural Diversity and Cultural Differences," in Ashcroft, Griffiths, and Tiffin, *Post-Colonial Studies Reader*, 208.

John Searle: The Constitutive Role of Language

In addition to the significance of mental capacities in language, John R. Searle took the study of language to a whole new level by emphasizing the constitutive role of language. Searle boldly claimed that everything including the existence of social institutions is birthed out of language.[43]

Searle first argued language is not only an expression of ideas, but a form of representation. Precisely, Searle calls that "Linguistic representation" which carries an intentionality of human beings vis-à-vis the state of affairs that is being represented.[44] In other words, Searle believes the purpose of language is larger than itself. Human beings "use meaning (semantics) to create a reality that goes beyond meaning."[45] Thus Searle continues, "Once you have the capacity to represent, you already have the capacity to create a reality by those representations."[46]

Language permeates all realities of a society, for "the reality of government, private property, and marriage as well as money, universities, and cocktail parties" and so on, are representations that are constructed essentially through language.[47] So Searle says, "Language doesn't just describe; it creates, and partly constitutes, what it both describes and creates."[48] In this socially constructed reality, one can "create" a kind of public discourse to mobilize others to act.[49] To illustrate what kind of action it is, Searle highlighted the aspect of deontology in language. Deontic powers refer to the kind of "powers such as those of rights, duties, obligations, requirements, and authorizations."[50] In explicating further the idea of public deontology, Searle says,

> We have a capacity to create a reality by representing it as existing. The only reality that we can so create is a reality of deontology. It is a reality that confers rights, responsibilities, and so on. However, this is not a trivial achievement because these right, responsibilities, and so on are the glue that holds human society together.[51]

---

43. Searle, *Making the Social World*, 62.
44. Searle, *Making the Social World*, 66–74.
45. Searle, *Making the Social World*, 64–65.
46. Searle, *Making the Social World*, 84–85.
47. Searle, *Making the Social World*, 84–85.
48. Searle, *Making the Social World*, 84–85.
49. Searle, *Making the Social World*, 84–85.
50. Searle, *Making the Social World*, 91.
51. Searle, *Making the Social World*, 89.

In short, when a reality is made up of all necessary linguistic representations, the reality provides reasons for public action and more than that, enables and obliges the public to act accordingly.

Two things are worthy of note. First, the concept that reality is socially constructed does not necessarily mean reality as a whole is merely an assemblage of words. Theorists of social constructionism, such as Chris A. M. Hermans, have made clear that "language is an important medium through which we understand and represent reality. But this does not mean that we can reduce reality to words."[52] Hermans highlighted the difference between "ontological objective" and "epistemological subjective" that Searle made, to substantiate his claim. Searle understands that a tree is a tree in which the existence of the tree is a fact that cannot be denied. Anything that is ontologically verified "is a reality corresponding to our statements."[53] What is contestable is not the existence of the thing, but the "description" that goes with it. How one describes a tree, including its shape, size, color, height and so on, and what that tree means to the person and others will make a huge difference. It is because the differences in constructing the reality reflect one's perception of the reality; to be more specific, the significance of "objective facts" varies from culture to culture. The value of the reality does not rest on an individual's statement, but the preexisting bias in language.[54] "No social reality exists unless it is given a linguistic meaning," as Hermans concludes.[55]

If, according to Searle, "A socially constructed reality presupposes a non-socially constructed reality,"[56] it leads to our second observation. The constitutive role of language is essential for not only constructing a social reality, but also regulating social relationships. In *The Construction of Social Reality*, Searle claimed that social behaviors have always been understood in collective terms. It is because the act of collective behaviors reflects the kind of collective intentionality that "is essential to understanding social facts."[57] Social facts are also known as institutional facts that represent "a structure of power relations, including negative and positive, conditional and categorical, collective and individual powers."[58] These powers can create meaning for members of the community in their daily living, regulate

---

52. Hermans et al., *Social Constructionism and Theology*, xvi.
53. Hermans et al., *Social Constructionism and Theology*, xvi.
54. Hermans et al., *Social Constructionism and Theology*, xvi.
55. Hermans et al., *Social Constructionism and Theology*, xvi.
56. Searle, *Construction of Social Reality*, 191.
57. Searle, *Construction of Social Reality*, 23–24.
58. Searle, *Construction of Social Reality*, 94.

relations between members of the community through an imposition of rights and obligations, and help members to achieve higher social status.[59] And Searle emphasizes,

> Let us constantly remind ourselves that the whole point of the creation of institutional reality is not to invest objects or people with some special status valuable in itself but to create and regulate power relationships between people. Human social reality is not just about people and objects, it is about people's activities and about the power relations that not only govern but constitute those activities.[60]

Institutional facts that are generated through linguistic representation may impact the formation of the community's identity. Whenever a biased intention occurs in and through language, that language can become destructive. Collective intentionality is the condition in which the minds of people join in pursuit of something together. When collective intentionality is motivated by self-serving purposes, this form of power possibly approves a lopsided reality in the name of maintaining the consensus of the people. The resulting facts about the world and the other being shared among members of the community may not truly represent the world and the other. Besides, it is a dynamic process in which one chooses the word and communicates that word with the community members who in return give consent to the use of that specific word. There are people who justify the use of hate speech against others; there are also occasions when people are not attentive to the harms done through words, because the derogatory connotation is embedded in the language. Searle did not make a specific remark about the negative consequence of collective intentionality in his work. He did, however, say that individuals who are directly involved in the community are well aware of the existing institutional facts.[61] Since they are living in those facts, they seldom challenge them. This phenomenon may explain why there is a continuation of the acceptance of the status (and perhaps the status quo as well).

---

59. Searle, *Construction of Social Reality*, 94–102.
60. Searle, *Construction of Social Reality*, 106.
61. Searle, *Construction of Social Reality*, 117.

George Lindbeck: Speak and Act in the Language of Faith[62]

The constitutive role of language is not completely foreign to Christianity. Language and religious meaning are closely connected. In his cultural-linguistic approach to the study of religion, George Lindbeck understood religion as "comprehensive interpretative schemes usually embodied in myths or narratives and heavily ritualized, which structure human experience and understanding of self and world."[63] Lindbeck puts forward the idea that the cultural-linguistic medium shapes the entirety of life, including thoughts and behaviors. To explicate his thesis, Lindbeck argues that the linguistic tradition in any given culture "comprises a vocabulary of discursive and nondiscursive symbols together with a distinctive logic or grammar in terms of which this vocabulary can be meaningfully deployed."[64] The entire linguistic system becomes a reality in which people live and act. Through interaction with one another, people's inner attitudes and feelings can be experienced and expressed. Inner experiences are derivative.[65]

Lindbeck believed Christian faith can neither rest on the cognitive-propositionalist framework (claiming doctrines as propositional truth, which leads to a diversity of realities), nor the experiential-expressivist model (emphasizing common religious experience). Lindbeck strongly disagreed with the suggestion that core experience is translatable and communicable in religiously pluralistic contexts. Lindbeck claims, "(T)he assertion of commonality becomes logically and empirically vacuous."[66] The experiential-expressive model fails to explain the process of identity formation and the difference in identity *per se* within respective religious traditions and belief systems. Two different cultural-linguistic traditions are never identical with one another. Though Lindbeck expected that different religions can make their truth-claims, he presumed the differentiation between ultimate truth and other truth-claims.[67] Any assertion that Lindbeck supports religious pluralism is a false impression.

62. Lindbeck, "Interview with George Lindbeck," 29.

63. Lindbeck, *Nature of Doctrine*, 18.

64. Lindbeck, *Nature of Doctrine*, 19.

65. Lindbeck, *Nature of Doctrine*, 20.

66. Lindbeck, *Nature of Doctrine*, 32.

67. Lindbeck identifies three types of truth, namely categorial, intrasystematic, and ontological. The first one refers to "grammar" or "rules of the game." They are categories "of which truth claims are made and expressive symbolism employed." Categorial adequacy can be thought of as real, but they "do not guarantee, propositional, practical, and symbolic truth." Putting it simply, religions can make meaningful statements, but those statements are not necessarily and propositionally true. Second, the intrasystematic truth is "the truth of coherence." Lindbeck says, our confessional language, such

Lindbeck maintains, "It is a communal phenomenon that shapes the subjectivities of individuals rather than being primarily a manifestation of those subjectivities."[68] If one does not acquire the skills in a given linguistic world, including language and symbols of a respective religion, one simply cannot understand another religion. In the case of Christianity, a Christian is a Christian who knows the language embedded in the narratives, rituals, symbols, and the like. So Lindbeck argues,

> To become a Christian involves learning the story of Israel and of Jesus well enough to interpret and experience oneself and one's world in its terms. A religion is above all an external word, a *verbum externum*, that molds and shapes the self and its world, rather than an expression or thematization of a preexisting self or of preconceptual experience. The *verbum internum* (traditionally equated by Christians with the action of the Holy Spirit) is also crucially important, but it would be understood in a theological use of the model as a capacity for hearing and accepting the true religion, the true external word, rather than (as experiential-expressivism would have it) as a common experience diversely articulated in different religions.[69]

Christians far and wide are included in the one church, the Israel-like Church, because of the common story. In other words, the kind of ecclesiology that espouses church-as-Israel will bring all churches together in unity. And since he was so much influenced by Hans Frei's *Eclipse of Biblical Narrative*, Lindbeck believed the narrative meaning of the stories about Jesus

---

as 'God is Three and One' or 'Christ is Lord' "are true only as parts of a total pattern of speaking, thinking, feeling, and acting. They are false when their use in any given instance is inconsistent with what the pattern as a whole affirms of God's being and will." The coherence cannot be measured by external standards, but the ones internally. Finally, the ontological truth means "that truth of correspondence to reality which, according to epistemological realists, is attributable to first-order propositions." Lindbeck also emphasizes, "A statement, in other words, cannot be ontologically true unless it is intasystematically true, but intrasystematic truth is quite possible without ontological truth." This explains why Lindbeck is so concerned with the condition that all narratives need to be consistent with the stories of Jesus. For Lindbeck, "Not only do the stories about Jesus define a singular concept of Lordship . . . this concept of Lordship— so a theology of the cross maintains—is alone adequate to what is indeed most lordly in reality" (*Nature of Doctrine*, 34–50). Because of the lordship of Jesus Christ that connects all parts of the Christian story, Lindbeck was able to avoid reducing truth to a set of propositions. Lindbeck is not interested in the question of what is truth, but how truth is understood and presented in a given religion and how truth is lived out and transmitted within the community of faith. See Thuesen, "George Lindbeck on Truth."

68. Lindbeck, *Nature of Doctrine*, 19.

69. Lindbeck, *Nature of Doctrine*, 20.

can bridge the gap arising from historical criticism and modern theology. The story along with the vocabulary of symbols and syntax is more than a set of propositional truths, but the medium for Christians to (re)connect the text and the world and to "make statements about reality."[70] It is the story that "determines the meaning of images, concepts, doctrines, and theories of the Church rather than being determined by them,"[71] Hence, the story can only be told by the people who are acting and being acted upon within the tradition. Basically, God's story becomes our story and our story witnesses to God's story.

Lindbeck's understanding of language and its relation to the Christian faith and identity have drawn criticism, including from those who advocate religious pluralism. I will come back to that in the following section.

Christian Mission: A Constructed Reality

For both John Searle and George Lindbeck, language is more than expressing an idea and a thought. They are indeed telling us language constitutes a reality, and for Lindbeck particularly, cultural-linguistic makes up the Christian identity. Based on the framework that Searle has outlined, conceptualizing Christian mission as a constructed reality will give us a new perspective on the operation of the entire missionary movement.

A Reality within the Reality

First of all, the examples of the subjugated I mentioned early in the chapter have already put to question the inviolability of Christian mission. Christian mission is crammed with human calculations. When language can be manipulated for vested interests, it is not difficult to relate Christian mission with the concept of social construction. Language informs our way of interacting with other social beings. This applies also to religious language that carries what Searle has called deontic powers. The deontology in Christian language confers obligations, responsibilities, and in the case of missiological exploration, it is the call to evangelize the world. The ensuing question concerns the kind of reality constructed for sustaining the entire enterprise. Simply put, can prevailing mission discourses shape Christian practice and missionary activity to the extent that gives fair judgment on self and better understanding of the other?

70. Lindbeck, *Nature of Doctrine*, 21.
71. Lindbeck, *Nature of Doctrine*, 42.

The conceptualization of Christian mission as a constructed reality also implies that the reality of Christian mission is only one of many other realities. There are various realties even in a single cultural context, whatever they are. Putting it in another way, the reality of Christian mission is a reality within Reality. As Raimon Panikkar argues, Reality is not an object to be scrutinized and subdued.[72] In *The Rhythm of Being*, Panikkar states clearly that reality is like a "rhythm" that *intra*-connects things and events, and Panikkar coins it the "indwelling of all in all."[73] Building on Panikkar's understanding of Reality, truth is experienced when one participates in the Reality for the Reality. Knowledge to the Reality is accordingly a kind of knowing; knowing is a process meaning *getting to* know.

While no one can fully comprehend the Reality, Christian mission functions to discover and prepares people to be awed by the wonders of God. The statement can be summarized in C. S. Song's conviction that we are only "tracing the footsteps of God." Song suggested that once we give up the certainties that we hold onto by filling our faith with all "correct" answers, we are able to see "who we are" and appreciate the "personal encounter with that loving power we call God—from whose eternity we came and to whose eternity we return."[74]

Knowing that the reality of Christian mission is one reality helps transcend our minds and enables us to see our finiteness; meanwhile, it also relativizes the metanarrative that is well established, abiding, and popularly affirmed by Christians and missionaries. When churches and Christians reconnect with other realities, they will be able to find a better way to relate to others. Christian imperative in the renewed and reconstructed reality can mean to resist the temptation to save and to civilize the other, but instead to infuse new energies into the concerns shared with the other. Though mission, in this sense, is largely a human enterprise, the term "human enterprise" does not negate any sacred meaning in its intent or divine intervention in its operation. It does spell out clearly the creative expressions of humanity's work while attending to God's mercy and justice for the world.

---

72. Raimon Panikkar was ordained to the Catholic priesthood and held three doctorates—one in philosophy, the second in chemistry, and the third in theology. In 1954, he made his first trip to India. There Panikkar studied Indian philosophy and religion at the University of Mysore and the Banaras Hindu University. Panikkar was one of the theologians who helped draft the document *Nostra Aetate* of the Second Vatican Council. *Nostra Aetate* is the declaration on the relation of the Church to non-Christian religions. Panikkar, *Rhythm of Being*, 2.

73. Panikkar, *Rhythm of Being*, 45.

74. Song, *Tracing the Footsteps of God*, 7.

The Danger of Turning One Narrative into the Reality for All

A contrasting scenario arises when the reality of Christian mission is considered the Reality. This kind of undertaking easily results in constructing a biased reality in which one is against another. Making Christian mission relevant in today's world unfortunately entices people to a reality with a limited vision of the good news: Christianity, alone, has the Truth to tell. This is exactly what we have noticed in Lindbeck's proposal.

Let us come back to Lindbeck's cultural-linguistic approach. Lindbeck believed Christians who use a common language will share the same religious experience. The same language helps shape the Christian way of life, including naming God, thinking about God and worshipping God. It is also this specific language that determines how the story of God is understood. This language centers on the role of Jesus who "fulfills and transforms the overall biblical narratives of creation, election, and redemption, and thereby specifies the meanings of such concepts and images as Messiahship, Suffering Servanthood, Logos, and Divine Sonship."[75] As the summation of Israel's history, everything else is understood in light of him. Therefore, Lindbeck concludes "through Christ, Israel is prototypical for the Church . . . in being shaped by the story of Christ, the Church shares (rather than fulfills) the story of Israel."[76]

Lindbeck might have successfully created a reality that is mediated through language, but the reality of Christianity becomes totally dependent on the overarching theme of salvation. When the reality is dominated by this metanarrative, Christians rely on this reality to give them meaning, empower them, and enable them to differentiate themselves from non-Christians. The fixedness of this Christian identity can cause a wide-range of problems for missionary endeavors. The moment when Christians believe the metanarrative is the reality, the metanarrative itself gives people permission to do everything that includes compelling others to live in the one and only reality. I am not saying that Lindbeck tries to reduce truth to some fixed and rigid principles, which is what Lindbeck himself disagrees. I am more concerned with other narratives hidden in the metanarrative. In Robert Warrior's essay, "Canaanites, Cowboys, and Indians," he unveils two opposing perspectives narrated by two conflicting communities who name themselves the people of God.[77] One is the narrative of conquest and

75. George A. Lindbeck, "The Story-Shaped Church: Critical Exegesis and Theological Interpretation," in Fowl, *Theological Interpretation of Scripture*, 41.

76. Lindbeck, "Story-Shaped Church," 43.

77. Robert Allen Warrior, "Canaanites, Cowboys, and Indians: Deliverance, Conquest, and Liberation Theology Today," in Treat, *Native and Christian*, 93–104.

the other the narrative of the Canaanites. Warrior unwaveringly points out Native American Christians read themselves into the experience of the Canaanites. Given the years of oppression that Native American Christians suffered in their land, it is necessary to call Lindbeck's postliberal biblical interpretation into question. On the one hand, we are told that Jesus fulfilled the history of Israel; on the other hand, Lindbeck was silent to Israelites' violence against the Canaanites. As the summation of Israel's history, is Jesus to be associated with the oppressor? Regarding Israel's story as singular runs the risk of depreciating the multiplicity of voices in the text. The notion of a singular and unified biblical narrative does not treat each community of God fairly and hence do justice to the oppressed. Whose voice is to be preserved? Who has to be cast out?

Furthermore, treating cultural-linguistics as a system of its own may inevitably lead to conflicts with the religious other. When Lindbeck says that "the biblical world absorbs other worlds," the absorption language unavoidably presupposes an imposition of values, attitudes, and beliefs. David Jenson accurately stated the weakness of Lindbeck's proposal by challenging his narrow view about other cultures and languages. Jenson says,

> Lindbeck's view of the regulative view of doctrine, however, becomes problematic as soon as he turns his eyes to the question of communal identity in a wider world. His focus, in some respects, is communally introspective, yielding much fruit for intra-Christian witness, but little in terms of the Christian community's engagement with a wider, religiously pluralistic world. . . . Doctrine, in this sense, is regulative only for those who share it. It can be appreciated and engaged fully only by those who have been nurtured and sustained by its familiar strains and cadences. Though such acknowledgement prevents Christians (and others) from imposing their language upon others, it also tends to shift the focus away from those who speak religiously different languages.[78]

Whereas Lindbeck is convinced that Christianity alone is true categorically, intrasystematically, and ontologically, David Brockman critiques Lindbeck's approach as one that only reinforces the already known "knowledge" within the insiders' religion.[79] Brockman continues, "If religions truly are mutually untranslatable and incommensurable, then the terms and experiences of one religion are excluded from, and incomprehensible

78. Jensen, *In the Company of Others*, 181.
79. Brockman, *No Longer the Same*, 87–88.

within, another religion. Thus from within a given religion, all other religions are truly void."[80]

To be fair, I should say that Lindbeck is a proponent of interreligious dialogue. He even believes different religions have "incommensurable notions of truth," which means that other religious claims can be true in their own right. The problem is God's salvific act in Jesus Christ remains the standard to evaluate other religions. Lindbecks says,

> The missionary task of Christians may at times be to encourage Marxists to become better Marxists, Jews and Muslims to become better Jews and Muslims, and Buddhists to become better Buddhists (although admittedly their notion of what a "better Marxist," etc., is will be influenced by Christian norms). Obviously this cannot be done without the most intensive and arduous conversation and cooperation.[81]

Interreligious dialogue functions to "benefit other religions." It becomes obvious that Lindbeck holds tightly to the conviction of "no salvation outside the church." While his presumption entails a common goal of salvation for all world religions, it necessitates conversion of the religious other and their conformity to the Israel-like church. This is exactly the question: How do we explain the conversion experience of the religious other and the change of religious language? People of other religious convictions are required to pick up the Christian language and acknowledge the lordship of Jesus Christ in order to attain salvation, even though they do not understand salvation the same way as the Christians do. In other words, they are asked to abandon the language that represents them. Is it possible for one to unlearn one's language before acquiring the Christian language, if the old language has shaped the entire life of that person? Lindbeck contradicts himself, for he has ascertained that religious languages are untranslatable.

Based on Lindbeck's vision of the one church, Christians are living in an enclosed-world, speaking a language that is understood among them. And since interreligious dialogue is conditional, it functions to "benefit other religions." The community offers a low or limited level of engagement with the other. There is a chance that the Christian community will become inward-looking. The Christian community will show a high tendency of being narcissistic which implies that the community is less sympathetic to other realties but to preserve and defend their extravagant self-views. These community characteristics will have negative consequences for the future of Christian mission.

80. Brockman, *No Longer the Same*, 88.
81. Lindbeck, *Nature of Doctrine*, 54.

When we encounter another linguistic system, we encounter other visions of life. Will we allow ourselves to be open and be challenged by a different culture and a different reality? Do we see the need to expand our language of understanding God and the world? What kind of space is given for people who speak other languages than the ones dominating the world? Unfortunately, these rhetorical questions are often met with negative responses without ambiguity. The dominant Anglo-European languages fail to destabilize the enterprise of Christian mission, here and now. These languages are prone to narcissistic tendencies meaning that they are thought to be completely independent. They have acquired necessary skills and conditions, so they do not need others' assistance and inputs. The fact that Christian mission is understood in the Anglo-European linguistic structures conveniently renders other languages less talented and their realities less intelligible. People coming from those cultures do not have a name. Perhaps, they do not deserve to be remembered and honored. They all look the same. They are labeled the other.

Power of Discourses: The Construction of Otherness for World Evangelization

The conception of the other has conventionally been focused on the unequal relationship between the privileged and the underprivileged. According to Jonathan Z. Smith, otherness "is a matter of relative rather than absolute difference. Difference is not a matter of comparison between entities judged to be equivalent, rather difference most frequently entails a hierarchy of prestige and ranking."[82] Otherness is constructed to objectify another person, and or a group of people so as to defend the oppressor's self identity and vested interests.

Constructing Otherness for World Evangelization

In the case of Christian mission, otherness is an essential component for civilizing mission. Demon-making and stereotyping are two common methods for the construction of otherness. Demon-making as a way of dealing with the other is more than rhetorical hyperbole. As Elaine Pagels says, even Satan "did not materialize out of the air."[83] Pagels argues, "Satan

82. Jonathan Z. Smith, "What a Difference a Difference Makes," in Neusner, Frerichs, and McCracken-Flesher, *"To See Ourselves as Others See Us,"* 15.

83. Pagels, *Origin of Satan*, xviii.

has, after all, made a kind of profession out of being the "other"; and so Satan defines negatively what we think of as human. The social and cultural practice of defining certain people as "others" in relation to one's own group may be, of course, as old as humanity itself."[84]

In tracing the origin of Satan, Pagels linked up with the conflict between the forces of good and the forces of evil. "This vision of cosmic struggle," Pagels contends, "derived originally from Jewish apocalyptic sources and was developed . . . by sectarian groups like the Essenes as they struggled against the forces they saw ranged against them."[85] Furthermore, this line of thought in regard to Satan runs through the Bible and the missionary movement. Pagels asserts,

> This split cosmology, radically revising earlier monotheism, simultaneously involved a split society, divided between "sons of light," allied with the angels, and "sons of darkness," in league with the power of evil. Followers of Jesus adopted the same pattern. Mark . . . tells the story of Jesus as the conflict between God's spirit and the power of Satan, manifest in the opposition Jesus encountered from evil spirits and evil people alike. Each of the gospels in its own way invokes this apocalyptic scenario to characterize conflicts between Jesus' followers and the various groups each author perceived as opponents . . . the movement became increasingly Gentile, converts turned thus sectarian vocabulary against other enemies—against pagan magistrates and mobs engaged in bitter struggle with the growing Christian movement, and against various groups of dissident Christians, called heretics—or, in Paul's words, "servants of Satan."[86]

In the history of Western Christianity, Pagels insisted that the fact that Satan was used "to represent one's enemies lends to conflict a specific kind of moral and religious interpretation, in which 'we' are God's people and 'they' are God's enemies, and ours as well."[87] Her observation resonated with what Edward Said has proposed that making statements about the other is a way to define one's own identity. The differentiation between Christians and the other is strengthened not only by social conventions but also linguistic creation. Registering someone with a label of "demon" becomes a precondition for rescuing and civilizing mission. Putting it bluntly, demonizing the other, however unwittingly, is unavoidable in Christian mission.

84. Pagels, *Origin of Satan*, xviii.
85. Pagels, *Origin of Satan*, 179.
86. Pagels, *Origin of Satan*, 179.
87. Pagels, *Origin of Satan*, xix.

Since the presumption that salvation has been brought forth by Western Christianity was deeply rooted, the thought that all non-Europeans
were "barbarians" became mainstream currency for churches particularly
in the Age of Exploration to problematize otherness. Non-Europeans or
simply barbarians were nothing but sinners "in need of salvation."[88] Paul
Hiebert points out,

> People were not humans to be known personally. They were ob-
> jects to be counted, analyzed, and reduced to general categories,
> laws, and theories. They were lumped into anonymous collec-
> tives in which particularities were eliminated by definition and
> broad generalizations formulated. The result was the theory of
> racial determinism and modern racism.[89]

The practice of dichotomizing cultures did not change much up to the
nineteenth century, and perhaps worsened. While missionaries advanced
the gospel to the land of heathens, they failed to challenge the ideology of
imperialism and recognize adverse effects of their own worldviews to the
indigenous culture. Frantz Fanon in *Black Skin White Masks* critiqued both
the colonial government and the former missionaries who were responsible
for inculcating the colonized with a sense of inferiority and shame of being
the other.[90] Fanon poignantly states, "However painful it may be for me to
accept this conclusion, I am obliged to state it: For the black man there is
only one destiny. And it is white."[91] For a black man to take in and to internalize an imposed identity as "dirty nigger" or "negro" is appalling.

To deem blackness or otherness as undesirable or anything less than,
evidently suggests that the Christian missionary movement is tantamount
to creating a reality to perpetuate white supremacy. Leon De Kock believes
otherness as a form of narrative is manipulated to foster "a master narrative
of Protestant conformity."[92] In Emmanuel Levinas's words, otherness functions to preserve the "imperialism of the Same."[93] The rationality not only
underlies the necessity of Christian mission, but also reinforces the white
man's burden.[94]

88. Hiebert, *Gospel in Human Contexts*, 64.

89. Hiebert, *Gospel in Human Contexts*, 68.

90. Fanon, *Black Skin, White Masks*, 10–13.

91. Fanon, *Black Skin, White Masks*, 12.

92. De Kock, *Civilising Barbarians*, 2.

93. Levinas quoted in Isherwood and Harris, *Radical Otherness*, 2.

94. Increasing numbers of theologians and historians from the majority world
are challenging both the notion of the white man's burden and the claim that Western Christianity is the prototype for other cultures. In *The Changing Shape of Church*

Apart from demonization, stereotyping is rampant upon missionary encounter. In her article titled "Do Muslim Women Need Saving?" Lila Abu-Lughod openly criticized the cultural stereotyping of Muslim women as a homogenous group of oppressed people. The life of Muslim women is traditionally portrayed as subservient, destitute, being abused and enslaved and the list goes on. Such categorization, however, does not do justice to the multiplicity of cultural identities and traditions across the Muslim world. On the one hand, the objectification of Muslim women necessitates the moral crusade and its rescue mission in liberating Muslim women from Islamicist oppression. On the other hand, Abu-Lughod pointed out that numerous Muslim women are highly educated salaried professionals particularly in Iran and in Egypt, but that fact is under-reported and most often deliberately ignored.[95] Leon de Kock, who is critical of Western intervention and particularly British colonialism in the construction of South African history and identity, defiantly asks, "Were the barbarians in need of civilising, or were the civilisers the true barbarians?"[96]

The Power of Discourses: Creating Binarial Relationships in Missionary Activities

Otherness does not exist in isolation. Otherness and the discourse on the other are closely connected. As the role of discourses is pivotal in the realm of Christian mission, what exactly are discourses? According to James Paul Gee,

> Discourses are ways of behaving, interacting, valuing, thinking, believing, speaking, and often reading and writing, that are accepted as instantiations of particular identities . . . by specific groups. . . . Discourses are ways of being "people like us." They are "ways of being in the world." They are "forms of life." They are socially situated identities. They are, thus, always and everywhere social products of social histories.[97]

History, Justo L. Gonzalez argues that "the map of the church has changed. . . . That is beginning to affect the reading and the writing of church history. . . . At the beginning of the century, the great missionary centers of Christianity were New York and London. Today more missionaries are sent from Korea than from London . . . growth in the North Atlantic has been much less spectacular" (Changing Shape of Church History, 9–16).

95. Abu-Lughod, "Do Muslim Women Need Saving?"

96. De Kock, Civilising Barbarians, 4.

97. Gee, Social Linguistics and Literacies.

Discourses are pervasive. They affect all aspects of life. Since discourses are ingrained with assumptions about *other*, the world, and even the conception of God, they can shape the way one lives in accordance with the assigned identity. At times and at worst, discourses can be divisive.

I have mentioned earlier that the problem of the other provides a major point of entry for dealing with the other. Esme Cleall has clearly stated that the language of difference is purposely selected to respond to specific social circumstances. Certain missionary agencies and societies were obsessed with the concept of difference to justify the behaviors done to potential believers.[98] Said summarized the phenomenon as an act of making statements about the other in order to exercise power over the other.[99]

Leon de Kock took it a step further to say that discourses on the other can both create and constitute the subjectivity of an individual. Discourses are, however, "the ideological 'interpellation' of the subject . . . or the discursive expression of particular interests masquerading as general wisdom."[100] In a similar vein, Judith Butler asserted that the coercive nature of power in a form of discourse influences the sense of self. Thus she says, "Subjection consists precisely in this fundamental dependency on a discourse we never chose but that, paradoxically, initiates and sustains our agency."[101]

In view of that, William Scott Green gave us a concrete example of how the internalization of values imposed by the higher authority is made possible through language. Green connected the "semantic component" to the task of constructing otherness. The semantic component started right from "the very act of naming" that accurately captures the power differential existing between the one who names and the one being named.[102] Green explained that those who are named something else, such as "crocodiles," passively receive the name given for them. On the one hand, if "crocodiles" denotes some kind of negative meaning in a given culture, the name carries with it the value judgment upon the other; on the other hand, the other's passivity implies a form of reaction to the imposition of value/value-laden identity. The people cannot get rid of that name, because the name is "an act of appropriation" by the majority in society.[103] So Green says, "A society does not simply discover its others, it fabricates them by selecting, isolating,

---

98. Cleall, *Missionary Discourses of Difference*, 3.

99. Said, *Orientalism*, 2.

100. Kock, *Civilising Barbarians*, 11.

101. Butler, *Psychic Life of Power*, 2.

102. William Scott Green, "Otherness Within: Towards a Theory of Difference in Rabbinic Judaism," in Neusner, Frerichs, and McCracken-Flesher, *"To See Ourselves as Others See Us,"* 49.

103. Green, "Otherness Within," 50.

and emphasizing an aspect of another people's life and making it symbolize their difference."[104] The construction of otherness may be as old as the bible, but we simply let this categorization go without confronting it. Missionary discourses and the betrayal of the missionized's agency are again enmeshed. One cannot bring justice to the missionized-other without interrogating missionary discourses.

Apparently, there exists in the discourse an inconsistency between what the thing (or a person) is and how the thing (or a person) is presented. This discrepancy, including but not limited to the intellectual, bodily, spatial, and affective dimensions, appertains to the content of the presentation. For Paul Riceour, it is concerned with who narrates. Anyone can speak, but not everyone can create an impact on the other through the narrative. Ricoeur introduced us also to the concept of selfhood in which self speaks without any reference, and the narrative that self creates has to do with presenting "the moral subject of imputation."[105] The one who narrates can powerfully create a condition that makes known the hidden moral standard and judgment, but that also is constitutive of the community's identity.

Discourses and the Production of Truth

How do we know the narration is authentic without jeopardizing local culture and disgracing local wisdom? How do we know which narrative is true when the story gets told in different ways? I find Michel Foucault's analysis of discourses highly relevant to our discussion. Foucault expressed concerns about the close connection between discourses and the production of truth.[106] Things that were said before and how they were said could become truth. Foucault says,

> Well, it is the interest I have in modes of discourse, that is to say . . . we live in a world in which things have been said. These spoken words in reality are not, as people tend to think, a wind that passes without leaving a trace, but in fact, diverse as are the traces, they do remain. We live in a world completely marked by, all laced with, discourse, that is to say, utterances which have been spoken, of things said, of affirmations, interrogations, of discourses which have already occurred. To that extent, the historical world in which we live cannot be dissociated from all the elements of discourse which have inhabited this world and

104. Green, "Otherness Within," 50.

105. Ricoeur, *Oneself as Another*, 169.

106. Foucault, *Power/Knowledge*, 117.

continue to live in it as the economic process, the demographic, etcetera, etcetera.[107]

Foucault makes clear that truth is already made available for us before we know it. He maintains that "history has no 'meaning' . . . one's point of reference should not be to the great model of language (*langue*) and signs, but to that of war and battle."[108] History does not speak. It is the language of humanity that does. For Foucault, it is necessary to question the mechanism that governs a statement and the validation of it.[109] Therefore Foucault takes on the formation of scientific "discourses" along with the practice of power in the history of Western civilization.[110]

In his analysis of power, Foucault observes,

> What makes power hold good, what makes it accepted, is simply the fact that it doesn't only weigh on us as a force that says no, but that it traverses and produces things, it induces pleasure, forms knowledge, produces discourse. It needs to be considered as a productive network which runs through the whole social body, much more than as a negative instance whose function is repression.[111]

It is precisely the fecundity of power that produces things, including but not limited to truth. According to Foucault, truth is not of divine origin as people used to think. It is an inevitable product of power. The objectivity of truth depends on the discourse of truth that goes along with it. Discourses embedded with power govern the way knowledge is formed. In other words, truth expresses itself in the form of knowledge that we agree on. Knowledge immediately shapes social behaviors and relations operated in politics, international relations, and even the expansion of Christianity.

Discourses, as Foucault repeatedly points out, are the indispensable constituent of "the internal regime of power" even though the discourses may not be true in themselves.[112] We inherited a world in which knowledge has been formed, and that kind of knowledge becomes universal and continues to guide our thinking and actions. Foucault thus considers the regime of power within a historical framework as "genealogy." For that, Foucault means, "a form of history which can account for the constitution

107. Foucault quoted in Chow, *Not Like a Native Speaker*, 53.

108. Foucault, *Power/Knowledge*, 114.

109. Foucault, *Power/Knowledge*, 112–13.

110. Foucault, *Discipline & Punish*, 23.

111. Foucault, *Power/Knowledge*, 119.

112. Foucault, *Power/Knowledge*, 112–18.

of knowledges, discourses, domains of objects etc., without having to make reference to a subject which is either transcendental in relation to the field of events or runs in its empty sameness throughout the course of history."[113] Discourses operating in the realm of genealogy allow preconceived knowledge to infiltrate systems and institutions on all levels. The genealogy of knowledge explains how things work and how relationships are formed in the history of humanity.

The pervasiveness of power further implicates the connivance of truth-making. Even Christianity has long been shaped by the thought-forms and worldviews of a specific group of people and cultures.[114] Western epistemological categories, including values and how those are conceptualized in respective linguistic traditions, become absolutely correct. Thus Hamid Dabashi challenged the rationality that determines what counts as knowledge and what not. So he asks, "Why is it that a Mozart sneeze is 'music' . . . but the most sophisticated Indian music ragas are the subject of 'ethnomusicology'?"[115] He found it disgraceful that those who do not come from the "European philosophical genealogy" and those who do not "practice their thinking in the European languages they have colonially inherited" are not given the opportunity to make knowledge more valuable and significant to humanity and the world as a whole.[116] Their languages, cultures and realities are generally associated with "ethnic." Things that are ethnic-related are not primary and they are of other interests. In Hamid Dabashi's words, they are simply "the subject of Western European and North American anthropological fieldwork and investigation."[117]

Talad Asad's skepticism about history making is very much along the lines of Foucault and Dabashi on challenging the process of truth-making in Western cultural frameworks. Asad is however more sophisticated in analyzing the impact of the West on non-Western societies. In his interrogation of the practice of "systematicity" that includes the accumulation of data about the local people and the scrutinization of that, Asad believed that kind of system can never "mirror" the people.[118] They remain a group of representatives. Thus Asad promptly questioned the idea of local understood as local people and local history, because that kind of arbitrary delineation is based on the genealogy of Western knowledge. That only strengthens the

---

113. Foucault, *Power/Knowledge*, 117.

114. Cf. Smith, *Meaning and End of Religion*, 80.

115. Dabashi, *Can Non-Europeans Think?*, 32.

116. Dabashi, *Can Non-Europeans Think?*, 30–31.

117. Dabashi, *Can Non-Europeans Think?*, 32.

118. Asad, *Genealogies of Religion*, 7.

connection between "power and subjection."[119] Asad points out that "pre-defined social relations and language forms, as well as the body's materiality, shape the person to whom 'normal' desires and choices can be attributed. That is why questions about what it is possible for agents to do must also address the process by which 'normal persons' are constituted."[120]

The Need for Constructive Discourse on the Other and Otherness

At this point, discourses are largely analyzed in negative terms. It is understandable but it is not necessary to demonize the discourse on discourses. Let me come back to Foucault's discussion of discourses. When saying Foucault is concerned with the way discourses give guidance to people's thoughts and acts, Foucault never means to abandon discourses. It is near to impossible, since as Foucault believed discourses are ubiquitous. Moreover, discourses are not inherently evil. What Foucault opposed is the destructive side of discourses. Foucault wanted to see a form of communication that brings justice and righteousness to society. Thus Foucault says people need to take notice of "the production of truth." Foucault continues, "It's not a matter of emancipating truth from every system of power (which would be a chimera, for truth is already power) but of detaching the power of truth from the forms of hegemony, social, economic and cultural, within which it operates at the present time."[121] When people refrain from privileging themselves at the expense of others, it will make possible what Foucault has called "the possibility of constituting a new politics of truth."[122]

Apparently no discourse is ever complete. Luce Irigaray also puts it, "A discourse can poison, surround, close off, and imprison, or it can liberate, cure, nourish and fecundate. It is rarely neutral. Even if certain practices strive for neutrality in language, it is always just a goal, or a tangent, and never reached; it is always to be constructed."[123] What matters is to conceptualize anew the conceptions of self and other in missionary discourses. If that is the case, the aspect of power relationship and its validity should give a new dimension for an analysis of the relationship between Christians and non-Christians. For the purpose of methodological discussion, Foucault's argument of the production of truth leads us to reflect on the reality

119. Asad, *Genealogies of Religion*, 13.

120. Asad, *Genealogies of Religion*, 13.

121. Foucault, *Power/Knowledge*, 133.

122. Foucault, *Power/Knowledge*, 133.

123. Irigaray, *To Speak Is Never Neutral*, 4–5.

in which Christians live and witness. It should also force us to critically evaluate the language crafted in missionary endeavors, including missionary formation and leadership.

Summary

Language can shape our worldview and create ethical demands and religious obligations. What a Christian says and how a Christian interacts with people of other cultures matters in the missionary encounter. As the world continues to divide along—and even intensify the division of—geographical, religious, and racial lines, it is necessary to address the power differential in relationships.

Practices of othering through discourses and its normalization perpetuate a reality that potentially renders a specific group of people inferior. We tend to see the weakness of the other when evaluating the difference from one culture to another. We love to point out the problem of the other. If the narrative sounds familiar, it is because we are inheriting a reality that places an importance on erasing differences and turning the other into us. Inheriting is a major issue, because Christians simply take for granted the metanarrative that Christianity has the truth to tell, and willingly live in the reality shaped by that trajectory. The task of examining power and knowledge accumulated through genealogical ways will require us to tackle the ideology of self preserved in and through language for creating boundaries against the other.

The Christian mission enterprise can no longer assert its neutrality on the matter of language. Being inward-looking makes the Christian community more narcissistic and less sympathetic to other realties.

3

Mission Discourses and Otherness

IN THE PREVIOUS CHAPTER, I provided an analysis of the close connection between language and otherness. In this chapter, I want to show how biased perceptions in self actually happened in the history of modern Christian mission. Contrary to presenting meta-knowledge, I pursue the study of mission discourses with a contextualized approach. I will consider several types of mission discourses crafted for the purpose of world evangelization, in relation to the tendency to fetishize potential believers as cultural stereotypes. I will specifically draw on various well-known mission literature and publications, including William Carey's *An Enquiry*, reports on the World Missionary Conference in Edinburgh (1910), The WCC's *Guidelines on Dialogue with People of Living Faiths and Ideologies*, The Vatican's *Ad Gentes* and *Nostra Aetate*, and other modern mission documents. The selection of these examples is primarily due to their overwhelming impact on the orientation of mission understanding even in today's world. Revisiting past mission discourses is not necessarily a reinforcement of past achievements, but a critical reflection on past experiences and mistakes in order to create a possibility for better pathways in the discipline of missiology.

The Patterns of Change in Mission Discourses

Objectification does not exist in the abstract. It takes place mainly through the mediation of language. Foucault has warned us that discourses carry with them genealogies of knowledge and power, and the things said—whether they themselves are true or not—can turn into truth. While taking seriously the power of discourses, we need to understand that language is not static. Linguists generally believe language changes over time. John

McWhorter argues that "language . . . *is* change."[1] There is nothing we can do to stop the change, because change is not only affected by, but also is in response to socio-cultural and political circumstances. Noam Chomsky asserts that "language is innovative" which means each new discourse or sentence is "not a repetition of anything . . . heard before" but is modified and configured with a specific intention.[2] In a sense, the creation of a new reality will enable further changes to occur.

Understanding change as a natural part of language is very important for our investigation of mission discourses and their changing patterns. Mission discourses have gone through a process of mutations along the history of the Christian missionary movement. This section will basically cover two things: first, the shift of terminologies in interreligious relations, and second, the shift of terminologies in Christian service. The patterns of change in mission discourses will not only indicate what has been done, but also what has been left undone in our relationships with the other. We will also see how church leaders and theologians in the South question the civilizing mission, react to the very materiality of human life conceptualized in relevant mission discourses.

A Shift of Terminologies in Interreligious Relations: "Heathen," "Non-Christian," "People of Other Faiths," and "Neighbor"

William Carey: An Enquiry into the Obligations of Christians to Use Means for the Conversion of the Heathens

First of all, I will start with evaluating the mission of William Carey, in particular, his writing related to evangelical mission. His publication titled *An Enquiry* continues to be one major reference for the discussion of world evangelization. Not only missiologists of Western societies, but numbers of leaders from the majority world also find his work inspiring and a good model to follow.[3] How he described people who did not acknowledge the

---

1. John McWhorter, currently Associate Professor of English and Comparative Literature at Columbia University, argues that language is not static but dynamic. Language will continue to evolve in relation to social, cultural, and political developments in human history. McWhorter, *Power of Babel*, 16.

2. Chomsky, *Language and Mind*, 10.

3. In his article titled "Issues in the Short-Term Missionary Strategy," Byung-yoon Kim argued that William Carey started the first era of modern mission through stationing along the coastal areas of India. The adoption of a Western model was necessary for Asian churches to engage missionary work. Kim says, "Most Asian missions, unlike the Western missions, do not have proper field structures to implement mission endeavors.

lordship of Jesus Christ is still relevant for Christian mission in the twenty-first century.

William Carey (1761–1834) was born into a weaver's family in Northamptonshire, England. Carey started out as a shoemaker and became pastor of a small Baptist congregation. After reading the *Last Voyage of Captain Cook*, Carey felt an urge to propagate the gospel among the heathens. He treated the book not just as a story of personal journey, but as a spiritual need for humankind. In 1792, he published *An Enquiry into the Obligations of Christians to Use Means for the Conversion of the Heathens* to uphold the Christian missionary imperative. An immediate result of the mission document was the inception of the Particular Baptist Society for the Propagation of the Gospel Amongst the Heathen, later renamed the Baptist Missionary Society (BMS) in 1793.

Many Christians believe Carey's mission should deserve high praise. In addition to translating the Bible into Bengali and other Indian dialects, Carey founded the Serampore College, lobbied for the abolition of sati (widow burning) and education for women, and supported other social reforms. All these works eventually won him the reputation of "the father of modern missions."[4] By 1821, Carey and other missionaries in the area baptized over 1400 new converts. There might be a correlation between Bible translation and the surging numbers of Christian converts, but that is not my primary concern. I will instead provide a critical analysis of Carey's writing and his rationale for missionary work.

The *Enquiry* is an eighty-seven-page document, consisting of five sections. In its preamble, Carey urged the propagation of the gospel by first stating that God's people of previous generations failed to accomplish what had been entrusted to them. To make the case strong, Carey immediately pointed to the evils of the world. He specifies, "in the time of Abraham, gross wickedness prevailed . . . the progress of evil was not stopped, but the Israelites themselves too often joined with the rest of mankind against the God of Israel."[5] The urgency of bringing the salvation of Jesus Christ to the sinful world came along with Carey's dualistic worldview. The world,

---

The remaining tasks are urgent and extensive so we need to develop an effective field system" (Byung-yoon Kim, "Issues in the Short-Term Missionary Strategy," in Ma and Ma, *Asian Church and God's Mission*, 189).

4. William Carey was not the first Protestant missionary sent to India. Bartholomaeus Ziegenbalg grew out of the pietistic movement in Germany and was eighty some years earlier than Carey in starting missionary work there. Even Carey himself recognized the work of Ziegenbalg in his *Enquiry* (36). The debate over honoring Carey tends to center on the legacy of his work.

5. Carey, *Enquiry*, 4.

according to Carey, was divided into the "Christian world" and the "heathen world." It implies that anyone who is not a Christian is a heathen.[6]

Section I deals with "An Enquiry whether the Commission given by our Lord to his Disciples be not still binding on us." Citing Matthew 28:18–20, the Great Commission, Carey made clear that the obligation was binding on Christians. "Going" to preach the gospel to all countries of the world was a burning call, for there are many "fellow-sinners, who to this day, are lost in ignorance and idolatry."[7] Carey refuted the idea that the commission was given only to the apostles. Such a thought would only encourage church members to stay in their comfort zone, and that would further hinder the implementation of the obligation. To end the section, Carey contrasted the different living between his countrymen or the saved who had the means of grace, and the heathens "who have no Bible, no written language . . . no good civil government, nor any of those advantages which we have."[8] The comparison aimed to persuade his countrymen to engage the evangelization of the world. In other words, introducing the gospel to the people out there would instantly help them to become civilized.

In Section II, Carey presented "a Short Review of former Undertakings for the Conversion of the Heathen." Carey traced the history of evangelism back to the New Testament times. Great examples of missionary work were documented in the Acts of the Apostles, in particular Paul's four missionary journeys. Though Paul experienced tremendous difficulties even to the point of imprisonment, he remained "obedient to the heavenly vision."[9] The agenda of preaching Christ to the Gentiles was further justified by the examples of church fathers, such as Justin Martyr, Ireneaus, and Tertullian, and other contemporary missionaries. Their zeal in sowing spiritual seeds to the heathens would be a model for Christians of later generations to do likewise. Preaching Christ to the Gentiles should therefore top the list among other church agendas.

In connection with the sign of the times, Carey gives "a Survey of the present State of the World" in Section III. The survey included twenty-three

6. Heathen has different meanings in Carey's writing. One of them is associated with ignorance. Referencing Romans 1:21–23, Carey regards this kind of ignorance as wisdom that "*knew not God, but changed the glory of the incorruptible God* as much as in the most barbarous ages, *into an image made like to corruptible man, and to birds, and four-footed beasts, and creeping things*" (*Enquiry*, 4). Ignorance like that only results in "more abundant and extravagant idolatries" (*Enquiry*, 4). In that respect, Carey's missionary imperative is to eliminate ignorance that is rooted in one's unbelief in the lordship of Jesus Christ.

7. Carey, *Enquiry*, 8.

8. Carey, *Enquiry*, 13.

9. Carey, *Enquiry*, 23.

tables of statistical data detailing the population, civilization, and religion of many countries around the world. Carey unhesitatingly accepted the prevailing categorization of the world, namely, Europe, Asia, Africa, and America. He considered Christianity, Judaism, and Islam major religions of the world. Anything outside those categories are called pagan, and over half of the inhabitants in the world, in Carey's opinion, were still living in pagan darkness. These are the people who practice cruelties and immoralities with eagerness.[10]

Section IV discusses "the Practicabilty [sic] of something being done, more than what is done, for the Conversion of the Heathen." Carey first identified the benefits associated with growing commerce. Travel to the heathen land was no longer a problem, and missionaries would find it more convenient to reach out to the heathens, civilize them, and turn them into "useful members of society."[11] Carey also shared some concerns when engaging the heathens, such as the danger of being killed by cannibals, the way of sustaining oneself in mission, and the necessity of learning the language of the heathens. Despite all the challenges, Carey believed faithful missionaries would endure "hardness" and continue to find ways to be "good soldiers of Jesus Christ."

In the final section under the sub-heading of "An Enquiry into the Duty of Christians in general, and what Means ought to be used, in order to promote this Work," Carey argued prayer was necessary but not sufficient. He proposed the formation of a missionary society that was known as the particular Baptist denomination. A committee would be formed under the society to "procure all the information they could upon the subject, to receive contributions, to enquire into the characters, tempers, abilities and religious views of the missionaries, and also to provide them with necessaries for their undertakings."[12] Carey did not shy away from stating the need of money for the society's daily operation. Anyone who followed the biblical teachings about mission would eventually rejoice over the harvest of new Christians.[13]

The publication of The *Enquiry* helped disseminate Carey's vision particularly at a time when Westerners got interested in knowing and studying about other people and their cultures. His pioneering initiative of the institutionalization of a missionary society was also inspiring to his

---

10. Carey, *Enquiry*, 67.

11. Carey, *Enquiry*, 70.

12. Carey, *Enquiry*, 83.

13. Carey, *Enquiry*, 86.

contemporaries.[14] I am, however, taken aback by the assumptions lying behind Carey's mission rationale. Throughout the eighty-seven-page mission
document, heathens are referred to as "barbarous," "poor," and "uncivilized."
They are "ignorance," "cannibals," "pagans," and they practice "idolatry."[15]

What is more distressing is Carey's description of the heathens as
"scarcely human."[16] In his presupposition, the heathens are taken out of
their respective contexts and evaluated in light of the Christian framework.
This led to the dichotomization of the world, that is, the "Christian world"
and the "heathen world." Furthermore, the subsequent binary opposites
that include Christian/non-Christian and human/not-human are not independent of each other, but interconnected. Thus it means, Christian =
human and non-Christian = not-human. How do we possibly explain how
a life that is filled with God's spirit can dehumanize those who do not acknowledge the lordship of Christ? While preaching the good news is culturally conditioned, Carey was tempted to co-mingle missionary work with
the Enlightenment thinking. Evidently, it suggests that Christianization is
inseparable from civilization and Westernization.

The idea of heathenism is problematic. It has not much been taken
on in the evaluation of Carey's mission strategy. Recent Christian leaders
and missionaries continue to speak highly of Carey's achievements without
addressing his problematic worldview. Esme Cleall observes, "One of the
most pervasive tropes in missionary writing is the prevalence of 'heathen'
violence."[17] Heathen is not just about being a heathen, but is associated with
violence. Cleall goes on, heathens are those who practice "Cannibalism,
human-sacrifice, tribal warfare, circumcision, ritual suicide, hookswing-
ing, foot-binding, widow-burning, infanticide, self-flagellation and scarifi-
cation" and so on.[18] These descriptions of cruelty that largely focused on

14. The Lausanne Committee for World Evangelization (LCWM) selected Cape
Town as the location for hosting the International Congress on World Evangelization
2010, because the Committee wanted to honor William Carey who proposed the first
international missionary conference to be held there in 1810. The Rev. Dr. S. Douglas
Birdsall, LCWE Executive Chairperson, affirms, "We believe the 200th anniversary of
William Carey's vision and the centennial of its fulfillment is an appropriate time to,
once again, encourage international leaders to come together to chart the course for
the work of world evangelization in the twenty-first century" (Lausanne Movement,
"Cape Town 2010").

15. Carey, Enquiry.

16. Carey, Enquiry, 70.

17. Cleall, Missionary Discourses of Difference, 123–24.

18. Cleall, Missionary Discourses of Difference, 123. Cleall also observed that there
are different forms of heathenism. The scope of violence differs from context to context.
So she claims, "Whilst violence in Africa evoked 'heathen' disorder, in India, violence

the vulnerability of women and children remained prevalent throughout the nineteenth century. When the indigenous people act and behave in a way that fits the missionary's description of violence, their behavior is immediately tied to a deficit in their cultural and religious identities.

The way that the discourse construed non-Christians' identity is entirely negative. As heathenism became so disgusting, it justified coercive conversion of the heathens. It was tempting for missioner to predicate the evangelization of the world on the dehumanization of the other. The strategy of racialising indigenous people thus gained popularity. For instance, the *Women's Missionary Magazine* published in India during British colonial governance used to make racist statements, and from time to time, the magazine discussed "how the 'heathen' could be reached when they were so dark, so corrupt and so many, while the missionaries . . . were so white, so pure and so few."[19] Articles published in the magazine turned out to be a means to solicit more funds for the mission enterprise. Esme Cleall also points out that "depictions of violence woven between prosaic discussions of school-building and preaching kept missionary accounts vivid and made fundraising easier."[20]

Early mission discourses tend to suggest that Christianity could solve every problem brought by heathen violence.[21] These discourses identified Christians as the chosen people who were beneficiaries of God's special favor. That is why Cleall mentions how "Christian love" associates with the intent to emancipate victims.[22] The connection further fuels the narrative that "Christian love" is an answer to "heathen cruelty." If rhetoric is so formulated in a manner to persuade Christians to win souls, the discursive technique functions to provoke emotions and increase support for that specific cause. Inclusion is narrowly defined in an exclusive framework that justifies proselytization as a condition for the extension of God's love. When the dichotomization and hierarchical order of the world are so naturalized in people's perception of the world, this kind of worldview only perpetuates white supremacy, thus the ideology of exclusion.

---

was principally constructed through 'heathen' *civilisation*" (*Missionary Discourses of Difference*, 132).

19. Marcella Maria Althaus-Reid, "In the Centre There Are No Fragments: Teologias Desencajadas (Reflections on Unfitting Theologies)," in Storrar and Morton, *Public Theology for the Twenty-First Century*, 371.

20. Cleall, *Missionary Discourses of Difference*, 124.

21. Cleall, *Missionary Discourses of Difference*, 124.

22. Cleall, *Missionary Discourses of Difference*, 132.

The 1910 Edinburgh Conference: "Opportunity" to Evangelize
the Whole World

The World Missionary Conference (1910) was one of the early attempts summoned specifically for the evangelization of the world. The Conference primarily represented the interests of Protestant mission agencies and societies. It was clearly stated, in the Commission of Carrying the Gospel to All the Non-Christian World, that "the missions of the Roman Catholic and Russian Orthodox Churches" were not included in the report.[23] Besides, only 17 out of the 1400 delegates came from the non-Western world. The World Council of Churches admits, "The Edinburgh conference generally reflected a traditional conservative approach to mission, linking the proclamation of the gospel to the heathens with the spread of Western civilization."[24]

The underlying tone of the 1910 Edinburgh Conference was similar to that of Carey's in several respects, but its scale was much greater and the discussion more sophisticated. Like Carey's *Enquiry*, the publications of the 1910 Conference provided convincing reasons for the why, what, and how questions in regard to missionary endeavors of its time.

There was also a shared sense of urgency to take action for world evangelization. Its similar rationale highlighted the tension between Christian imperative and the failure to implement that. John Mott says, "It is a startling and solemnizing fact that even as late as the twentieth century, the Great Command of Jesus Christ to carry the Gospel to all mankind is still so largely unfulfilled. . . . The church is confronted today, as in no preceding generation, with a literally worldwide opportunity to make Christ known."[25]

The unsatisfactory fulfillment of the Great Commandment was nonetheless followed by a high degree of optimism. Church leaders and missionaries saw the world prior to the First World War full of opportunities. They even considered the time "wonderful." Thus the Commission was excited to declare

> The whole world is remarkably accessible. Improved means of communication have within the past two decades been spread like a great network over nearly all of the great spaces of unevangelised world, or are to-day being projected over these regions. For example, railway lines are being rapidly extended in different

23. World Missionary Conference, *Report of Commission I*, 3.

24. The Edinburgh Conference 1910 was a major contributing factor to the establishment of the International Missionary Council (IMC) in 1921, which was later integrated into the Commission on World Mission and Evangelism (CWME) in 1961 at the New Delhi Assembly. The IMC ceased to operate since that time. See WCC, "History."

25. Mott quoted in Galli, "Missions and Ecumenism."

sections of Africa, in the Levant, in Central Asia, in the Chinese Empire, and in the more populous parts of the East Indies, giving missionaries easy access to hundreds of millions of people. . . . One of the most significant and hopeful facts with reference to world evangelisation is that the vast majority of the people of the non-Christian nations and races are under the sway, either of Christian governments or of those not antagonistic to Christian missions. This should greatly facilitate the carrying out of a comprehensive campaign to make Christ known.[26]

This "wonderful opportunity" rhetoric failed to come with a right and just evaluation of the times. The Commission mentioned nothing about the harmful effects of colonization done to indigenous cultures, but focused only on the benefits of improved transportation and communication during the heyday of Western imperialism.

Obviously, Carey's conceptualization of the world continued to be a model for evaluating cultures and people of non-western societies. The task of categorization is dependent on how the world map is created, tabulated, and interpreted. Thus the *Statistical Atlas of Christian Missions* that the Commission prepared included maps of all missions in the non-Christian world. Based on "a more scientific study of the fields and problems," as it was said, the Atlas was meant to "impress the Church" and instigate fervor for effective world evangelization. Even today, the production of the Atlas, including the figures of global distribution of Christians and adherents of other world religions, is still significant among the evangelical circles. Obtaining comprehensive data means that they can analyze and predict religious demographics, so that churches can formulate mission strategy accordingly.

One noticeable change throughout the publication was the choice of word. The language of "heathen" was largely replaced by "non-Christian world" or "non-Christian religions" in the World Missionary Conference (1910). The term was not completely removed in the document. As the dichotomization of the world was foreseeable in the Christian-centric worldview, the idea of heathenism remained. Heathen repeatedly referred to uncivilized non-Western and non-Christian cultures and people. Despite the shortcomings of a dualistic worldview, a majority of missionaries and Christian leaders found the mission discourses appealing. The change in terminology did not lead to a change in perception toward the other. The egotistical tendencies remained active throughout the entire mission enterprise. Missionaries were entrusted with the task of educating anyone who

26. World Missionary Conference, *Report of Commission I*, 5–6.

was not a Christian, so that their "ignorance, prejudice, and superstition" could be removed.[27] One missionary account stated that "the women of India of various castes are coming to have a realising sense of their needs, and are seeking for education and light."[28] And it continued to say that those in "Pagan Africa . . . are awaiting the arrival of messengers."[29] People advocating for their rights and freedom is certainly a good thing, but the attempt to seize and turn the people's aspiration into a burden of the West is an inexcusable offense. Its underlying tone is self-centric, because missionary work continues to stress that "we" are commissioned to save those heathen souls who are still dwelling in darkness.

While the triadic relations of Christianization, Westernization, and Civilization entangled in a web of interlocking interests, the Commission was aware of the corrupting and demoralizing influences that came along with Western culture. There was in the report "a typical expression of the opinion of a great multitude of Asiatics and Africans," who protest,

> You come to us with your religion. You degrade our people with drink. You scorn our religion, in many points like your own, and then you wonder why Christianity makes such slow progress among us. I will tell you: It is because you are not like Christ.[30]

In response to the challenge, the Commission was convinced that only the spirit of Jesus Christ could effect changes to both Christian nations and the non-Christian world. The Commission affirms, "The missionary forces cannot win the non-Christian world for Christ until Christian nations and the new world movements of all kinds are more thoroughly permeated with the spirit of Christ."[31] The conviction that Jesus Christ is the answer to all human problems did not require the Christian nations to perform sincere repentance. This was sickening to the non-Christian world. Leon De Kock was strongly opposed to the violence of Westernization that came along with missionary activities. He criticizes,

> The vehicle of this "world mission" was an English which bore terrible certainties and was seldom tolerant of alterity. It was a language of closure and myopia, yet it represented an empire which could cause great turbulence for those who would not respect its insistence on orthodoxy.[32]

27. World Missionary Conference, *Report of Commission I*, 7.

28. World Missionary Conference, *Report of Commission I*, 8.

29. World Missionary Conference, *Report of Commission I*, 9.

30. World Missionary Conference, *Report of Commission I*, 23.

31. World Missionary Conference, *Report of Commission I*, 25.

32. De Kock, *Civilising Barbarians*, 29.

In the meantime, it is fair to say that there was a growing sympathy for non-Christian religions. Being sympathetic was understood as no condemnation of non-Christian religions. The Commission did not say anything about whether or not these non-Christian religions were of equal validity with the Christian faith. Suggestions for missionaries to engage non-Christians attended to general matters, such as "study and get to know the native religion."[33] When adherents of non-Christian religions remained the subject of study, the venture of knowing the religious other became merely a preparatory work for conversion.

The International Missionary Council (IMC): Christian Messages and Other Religions

The zeal for Christian mission continued to grow after the 1910 Conference in Edinburgh. The creation of the IMC in 1921 carried on the legacy of Edinburg, and the institution convened several other world mission conferences before its integration with the World Council of Churches (WCC) in 1961 at New Delhi. Since missionary activities by then were mostly active in countries and regions inhabited by adherents of other religions, challenges coming from these continents did force theologians, missionaries, and church leaders to rethink their approach to mission in religiously pluralistic contexts. How Jesus Christ relates to non-Christians, their cultures and religions became central to missiological discussion, especially at the Jerusalem Meeting in 1928 and the Tambaram Meeting in 1938. On a side note, the term "non-Christian" used both as a noun and as an adjective was prevalent in the two mentioned meetings. It was not until the Whitby Conference (1947) that delegates decided to abandon the principle of geographical distinction to refer to the "Christian" and "non-Christian" countries. The "non-Christian" label assumes people of other faiths are homogeneous. Such a categorization of people is disrespectful to respective religious traditions. It also reinforces the ideology that Christianity is the proper religion and others not. David Bosch also admits that "the world can no longer be divided into 'Christian' and 'non-Christian' . . . we now live in a religiously pluralist world."[34] Christian mission should be evaluated in light in this fact of plurality.

The official statement of the Jerusalem Meeting tried to show esteem for other religions, which obviously had not happened at the Edinburgh

---

33. World Missionary Conference, *Report of Commission I*, 20.

34. Bosch, *Transforming Mission*, 3.

conference. The volume entitled *The Christian Life and Message in Relation to Non-Christian Systems of Thought and Life* recorded this statement:

> We rejoice to think that just because in Jesus Christ the light that lighteth every man shone forth in full splendor, we find rays of that same light where he is unknown or even rejected. We welcome every noble quality in non-Christian persons or systems as further proof that the Father, who sent His Son into the world, has nowhere left himself without witness. Thus, merely to give illustration, and making no attempt to estimate the spiritual value of other religions to their adherents, we recognize as part of the one Truth that sense of the Majesty of God and the consequent reverence in worship which are conspicuous in Islam; the deep sympathy for the world's sorrow and unselfish search for the way of escape, which are at the heart of Buddhism; the desire for contact with Ultimate Reality conceived as spiritual, which is prominent in Hinduism; the belief in a moral order of the universe and consequent insistence on moral conduct, which are inculcated by Confucianism; the disinterested pursuit of truth and human welfare which are often found in those who stand for secular civilization but do not accept Christ as their Lord and Savior.[35]

To read between the lines, acknowledging the lordship of Jesus Christ continued to be the standard to secure a life of abundance. In another report titled *The Jerusalem Meeting of the International Missionary Council*, it was written that "Dr. Speer opened the discussion on the Christian message, and he struck the right note when he spoke of Christ as the sufficient, absolute and final Saviour of the world."[36] When that exclusive language set the tone for the entire discussion, we could imagine how the meeting would go. But it was the way that people thought in the early twentieth century. We could not ask for more.

What made this meeting special though, was that the National Christian Councils in Asia and Africa were allowed to send their own delegates. They could give input to the subjects such as the Christian life and message in relation to non-Christian systems, religious education, the relation between the younger and the older Churches, the Christian mission in the light of race conflict, Christianity and the growth of industrialism in Asia and Africa, and the Christian mission in relation to rural problems.[37] It is

35. *Christian Life and Message* quoted in Netland, *Dissonant Voices*, 17.
36. Cash, "Jerusalem Meeting," 271.
37. Cash, "Jerusalem Meeting," 270.

noteworthy that Asiatic delegates were serious about connecting their lived experiences with Christian convictions. W. Wilson Cash writes, "Asiatic delegates affirmed, that the East is looking for a religion that brings with it spiritual experience and makes God not a theory for discussion but a reality in facing the complex life of to-day."[38] This statement could well summarize the concerns of Asian Christians in regard to the Christian life and witness in their pluralistic situations.

The Tambaram Meeting in 1938 took the issue of other religions very seriously. Debates focused on whether or not God's revelation was present in the beliefs of other religions. The Dutch missiologist, Hendrik Kraemer, who almost dominated the discussion at Tambaram, insisted that God's revelation was manifested in and through Jesus Christ alone. Also in his work entitled *The Christian Message in a Non-Christian World*, Kraemer expressed concerns about compromising the uniqueness of Christ upon engaging people of other religions. His strong reaction to the value of other religious traditions could not give a satisfactory answer to Christians representing vastly different contexts. A Chinese delegate, T. C. Chao, openly challenged Kraemer's view. According to Mark Heim's analysis, Chao "argued that the acts of God in Jesus Christ . . . could not be seen as a uniquely episodic presence of God in history. . . . Chinese sages were inspired by the same God who is fully revealed in Jesus Christ. . . . If Christians were to take history with full seriousness in God's plan of salvation, they would seek to understand the role of *all* people's history, including their religious history."[39]

Since Tambaram, Madathilparampil Mammen Thomas had urged Asian Christians to construct an "authentic selfhood" centering on the witness to Jesus Christ as opposed to borrowing and applying uncritically Western theological concepts and imperialist values to churches in Asia.[40] The self-identity of Asian churches has to take root in its own soil. In response to the cause of humanization, M. M. Thomas clearly states,

> The mission of the Church in this context is to be present within the creative liberation movements of our time which the Gospel of Christ itself has helped to take shape, and so to participate in them as to be able to communicate the genuine gospel of liberation from the vicious circle of sin and alienation, law and self-righteousness, frustration and death into the new realm of Christ's New Humanity where there is forgiveness and

38. Cash, "Jerusalem Meeting," 272.

39. Heim, "Mission and Dialogue," 341.

40. Thomas, "Assessment of Tambaram's Contribution," 390–97.

reconciliation, grace and justification, renewal and eternal life. It is this message that will liberate the liberation movements from the false spiritual structures of meaning based on idolatrous worship schemes of self-redemption, and thus redeem their creative impulses from self-destructive tendencies, enabling them to achieve their inner rationale of human emancipation.[41]

M. M. Thomas's "Salvation as Humanization" did not only speak against disgraceful practices of capitalism, but also signified an alternative way to justly and rightly relate to the others. Engaging people of other religions cannot be discussed in isolation, but connected with social issues in respective regions.

The Tambaram Meeting was unable to find common ground on Christian mission in the context of religious pluralism. As Mark Heim observes, "A look back at Tambaram 1938 cannot solve the tension between mission and dialogue any more than the meeting 50 years later could clearly point the way toward its future resolution."[42] Heim also points out that "mission and dialogue are parts of one issue, not two isolated and alternate or opposing special interests."[43] Christians who have constant interactions with adherents of other religions cannot agree more with the position stated. Missionary work is meaningless if it fails to communicate effectively with people of other faiths.

Guidelines on Dialogue with People of Living Faiths and Ideologies: Dialogue in Community

As the necessity of dialogue was brought to the fore, the World Council of Churches found it appropriate to witness to Christ among people of other faiths. I have mentioned briefly that the integration of the IMC with the WCC became effective in 1961. All programs and responsibilities of the IMC were taken over by The Division on World Mission and Evangelism (DWME) and its committee. In 1971, a new subunit, Dialogue with Men of Living Faiths and Ideologies, under the Programme Unit on Faith and Witness was formed. Official discussion on interreligious dialogue finally started in 1977 when a group of scholars and theologians met in Chiang Mai, and two years later in 1979, the WCC published the Guidelines on Dialogue with People of Living Faiths and Ideologies. By highlighting the theme

---

41. Thomas, *M. M. Thomas Reader*, 89–90.

42. Heim, "Mission and Dialogue," 343.

43. Heim, "Mission and Dialogue," 343.

of dialogue in community, these guidelines came to realize that the Christian community is part of the larger community. Even adherents of other faiths are in no way inferior to Christians. They are actually "neighbors" of the Christian community. Dialogue happens naturally when Christians and their neighbors share life together within a given community. As it is stated,

> As Christians live together with their neighbours of other faiths and ideological persuasions the emphasis has come to be placed not so much on dialogue itself as on dialogue in community. The Christian community within the human community has a common heritage and a distinctive message to share; it needs therefore to reflect upon the nature of the community Christians seek together with others and upon the relation of dialogue to the life of the churches, as they ask themselves how they can be communities of service and witness without diluting their faith or compromising their commitment to the Triune God. Such an enquiry needs to be informed both by a knowledge of different religions and ideologies and by insights gained through actual dialogues with their neighbours.[44]

The WCC was changing its entire approach to the subject matter. The words "mission" and "evangelism" were not much used throughout the entire document. Engaging people of living faiths in the form of dialogue was considered an effective way to witness to Christ, and its entire undertakings functioned to "confess Christ" in all places. According to the guidelines,

> The words "mission" and "evangelism" are not often used in this statement. This is not because of any desire to escape the Christian responsibility, re-emphasized in the Nairobi Assembly, to confess Christ today, but in order to explore other ways of making plain the intentions of Christian witness and service. Christian integrity includes an integrity of response to the call of the risen Christ to be witnesses to Him in all the world.[45]

In general, the guidelines gave an impression that engaging people of living faiths only created a platform to confess Christ. Because of that, the WCC published a revised version of the guidelines in 2002 and specifically highlighted the aspect of "relations" with people of living religions. As is clearly indicated in the Guidelines for Dialogue and Relations with People of Other Religions (2002),

---

44. WCC, "Guidelines on Dialogue with People of Living Faiths."
45. WCC, "Guidelines on Dialogue with People of Living Faiths."

> In recent year, member churches have requested new guidelines on interreligious relations and dialogue that address today's context. More than ever, we sense a growing need not just for dialogue with people of other faiths but for genuine relationships with them. Increased awareness of religious plurality, the potential role of religion in conflict, and the growing place of religion in public life present urgent challenges that require greater understanding and cooperation among people of diverse faiths.[46]

Building genuine relationships with people of other religions was an important theme of the revised guidelines. Indeed, Asia's cultural-religio heritage can date as far back as 5000 years BCE. South Asia alone is the birthplace of many world religions, such as Hinduism, Buddhism, Jainism, and Sikkhism. Relating to people of other faiths for Asian Christians is not an option, which means something one can opt for or opt out. Many Asian Christian communities have been living in the context of religious pluralism for centuries. Their neighbors are primarily adherents of other faiths. Christians and people of diverse religious traditions meet and greet one another in school, at the marketplace, and through day-to-day business. Christians and these so-called religious others are participating in one another's lives through regular social interactions.

Asian religious pluralism therefore differentiates itself from what has been understood as the Western discourse of pluralism. Stanley Samartha observes that many people in the West come to a *discovery* of the value of religious pluralism. This new discovery of the reality is largely based on an assumption that healthy interreligious relation is an asset for the foundation of a peaceful and better world. People in the East (or the two-thirds world) however, are experiencing a *recovery* of their own spiritual and cultural values after centuries of Western hegemony.[47] The different evolutionary story between Western and Asian contexts requires Christians of today to sincerely engage the life of the other.

Building relationships at a superficial level will create unnecessary stereotypes. Samartha continues to argue that a Christocentric missiology that focuses only on the salvation of Jesus Christ is an exclusive concept, for the cross leads to the understanding of God through Christ's ontological suffering. A narrowly defined Christocentric mission comes close to supporting a theology of Christomonism. The Spirit "*proceeding from the Father*, remains the Spirit of God." The Spirit is present in both the work of Jesus Christ

---

46. WCC, "Guidelines for Dialogue and Relations."

47. Samartha, *One Christ, Many Religions*, 9.

and the work of God for the sake of God's entire creation. Unhesitatingly, Samartha asks, "Should not the presence and work of the Spirit of *God* be recognized in creation and in the life of people of other faiths, both *before* and *after* Jesus of Nazareth?"[48]

The presence of others can energize the feast of the Kingdom and make it more joyful. Their presence does evangelize the church in a way that speaks against any domineering desire in relationships with the divine. Thus Samartha contends,

> The intra-Christian and inter-religious debates need to be constantly related to each other for the sake of mutual criticism and mutual enrichment. While the former is very necessary in order for Christians to sharpen their profile and define their identity in a religiously plural world, the distinctiveness of a religious community cannot be truly defined without reference to other communities of faith in God's oikoumene.[49]

From Missio Ad Gentes to Missio Inter Gentes

Not only the Protestant circles are debating the validity of other religious traditions, but the Catholic Church also has long been wrestling with the issue of religious pluralism. During the Second Vatican Council, Pope Paul VI presented to members a draft of the Declaration on the Relation of the Church to Non-Christian Religions. He boldly claims:

> The Catholic Church rejects nothing that is true and holy in these religions. She regards with sincere reverence those ways of conduct and of life, those precepts and teachings which, though differing in many aspects from the ones she holds and sets forth, nonetheless often reflect a ray of that truth which enlightens all men. Indeed, the Church proclaims, and ever must proclaim, Christ as "the Way, the Truth, and the Life" (John 14:6), in whom men may find the fullness of religious life, and in whom God has reconciled all things to himself (cf. 2 Cor 5:18–19).[50]

The Declaration was impressive to many at the Council, particularly when it came to the value of other religious traditions. Cardinal Bea states,

---

48. Samartha, *Between Two Cultures*, 148.

49. Samartha, *Between Two Cultures*, 146–47.

50. Paul VI, *Declaration on the Relation of the Church*, 10.

Concerning these (non-Christian religions) it is, as far as I know, the first time in the history of the Church that a Council has laid down principles in such a solemn way. It is of great importance that we realize the great weight of the matter. It concerns the more than one billion people who either have not yet come to the knowledge of Christ and his work of redemption, or do not acknowledge them. Nevertheless, they can be saved if they obey the command of their conscience.[51]

If we take a closer look, we will see that an affirmation of all religions is rather limited in scope. All religions are great and they can be true on their own rights, but their religious meaning and truth have nothing to do with the Church (or the Church has nothing to do with them). The conviction that Christ is the only way to the fullness of life does not speak to people of other religions. The Declaration failed to deepen the relations between Jesus Christ and world religions. This negligence posed a considerable problem for Asian churches and communities.

According to the Decree *Ad Gentes*, the mission activity of the Church should entail planting the Church in the land of the unbelievers. Planting is more than a physical act, but is involved with a sense of spiritual nourishment. As summarized in paragraph 6 of the Decree, planting means to preach the Gospel and proclaim Christ's incarnation, death, and resurrection to believers, new and old. The principle of "mission to the nations" was also justified. As it is written in paragraph 4,

> Christ sent from the Father His Holy Spirit, who was to carry on inwardly His saving work and prompt the Church *to* spread out. ... The Church was publicly displayed *to* the multitude, the Gospel began *to* spread among the nations by means of preaching. ... For it was from Pentecost that the "Acts of the Apostles" took again ... just as Christ was impelled *to* the work of His ministry by the same Holy Spirit descending upon Him.[52]

The concept of *missio ad gentes* (mission to the nations) received negative responses among Asian theologians. Jonathan Tan argues, "*missio ad gentes* presumes a classicist perspective with Europe . . . as the center of Truth, and sees the task of mission in terms of European missionaries belonging to mission societies or missionary religious orders radiating outwards from this center toward those regions where ignorance of the Truth

---

51. Paul VI, *Declaration on the Relation of the Church*, 79.

52. Second Vatican Council, "Ad Gentes" (emphasis added).

reigns."[53] The adoption of this concept entirely negated the value and wisdom of other religious traditions.

The Federation of Asian Bishops' Conferences (FABC) was founded to discuss the significance of contextual situations in the Church's mission practices and understandings, following the meeting with Pope Paul VI in Manila in 1970. The FABC has debated the urgency to change its missiological approach since 1974, the first FABC Plenary Assembly.

Moving from *missio ad gentes* (mission *to* the nations) to *missio inter gentes* (mission *among* the nations), the FABC took into consideration the issue of religious pluralism in Asia. The use of "among" aimed to emphasize that Christianity should not be placed above any other religions. This change was not just about grammatical corrections or changing the choice of prepositions in its documentation, but also represented a fundamental alteration in mentality and the perception of the religious other.

Immediately after FABC I, Bishops Institute of Social Action (BISA) II was issued, and its statement on pluralism laid down the blueprint for the agenda of all subsequent meetings on pluralism. Pluralism is not deemed as evil, but a necessity to move forward the proclamation of the gospel in the midst of contrasting viewpoints.[54] BISA II, article 10 says,

> Pluralism is a necessity once we work through the mediation of secular analysis and worldviews. This pluralism should not be a threat to our Christian unity, but on the contrary, a positive and creative sign that our unity is deeper than whatever the concrete technical analysis or viewpoints might show: a genuine value that emphasizes unity in diversity.[55]

The FABC affirms that God's Word and acts are present among Asian spiritualities. More than a peaceful co-existence of diverse and opposing worldviews, pluralism signifies a celebration of God's Spirit indwelling among God's peoples. Affirming that God is at work among Asian spiritualities does not necessarily water down the gospel truth and thus soften the proclamation of the gospel. The FABC still sees the proclamation as a

---

53. Tan, "Missio inter gentes," 88.

54. After the inception of the FABC, considerable changes have been made in response to the dynamic situations of Asia. Tan observes, "The FABC has eschewed all forms of religious exclusivism, perceiving religious pluralism as an innate and unique aspect of the Asian socio-religious landscape. . . . While others may consider the diversity and plurality of postmodern Europe and North America as challenges that the church has to confront and overcome, for the Asian bishops, the question is rather how the Asian local churches could find themselves at home with such diversity and plurality" ("Missio inter gentes," 70).

55. BISA II quoted in Tan, "Missio inter gentes."

central piece for engaging other spiritualities; however, it also makes clear that proclamation is by no means equivalent to proselytization. As it is clearly written,

> But the proclamation of Jesus Christ in Asia means, first of all, the witness of Christians and of Christian communities to the values of the Kingdom of God, *a proclamation through Christlike deeds.* For Christians in Asia, to proclaim Christ means above all to live like him, in the midst of our neighbors of other faiths and persuasions, and to do his deeds by the power of his grace. Proclamation through dialogue and deeds—this is the first call to the Churches in Asia.[56]

Tan insists that "the FABC's preferred missiology is one of a 'mission *among* the nations' *(missio inter gentes),* with an emphasis on solidarity and harmony with the Asian peoples within their diverse and pluralistic *Sitz im Leben.*"[57]

Although the official discourse of the Church remains unchanged, the FABC and its determination to uphold the uniqueness of Asian churches have gained the respect of others. In *Redemptoris Missio,* an attempt known as renewing the Church's mission commitment, Pope John Paul II instructed the Church with specific directions to the South and the East. The instruction suggested that witness was an important part of the Church's evangelization.[58] About two years before the Encyclical Letter of Pope John Paul II in relation to the Church's mission, the Pontifical Council for Interreligious Dialogue formally replaced the Secretariat for Non Christians instituted under the leadership of Pope Paul VI. To adjust Roman Catholic thinking about other religious traditions, dialogue is adopted as an appropriate method to promote "mutual growth and enrichment."[59] It can never be used to proselytize.

The move from identifying those who do not acknowledge the lordship of Jesus Christ as "heathens" or scarcely human (as in Carey's word) to considering them "people" of other faiths does not come easy. The most basic step requires one to confess the wrong done to the other in the name of Christianity. How many Christian leaders will apologize for the dehumanizing speech and acts inflicted on others, especially when those mistakes were done by their predecessors? How many will risk a possible institutional sabotage upon encountering the wisdom of the other?

56. FABC quoted in Tan, "Missio inter gentes," 74.

57. FABC quoted in Tan, "Missio inter gentes," 84.

58. John Paul II, *Encyclical Letter Redemptoris Missio,* 71.

59. Vatican, "Pontifical Council for Interreligious Dialogue."

Nowadays, most mission societies and agencies are beginning to incorporate interreligious dialogue into their new mission strategy or mission program. My hunch is that many follow the current trend of Christian mission, partly because they see the promises for evangelization and partly because they are eager to remove from them the imperialist tag that has long been attached on them.

If the core understanding of religion in interreligious dialogue has not been changed, there will be no meaningful interaction with one another. Nile Green and Mary Searle-Chatterjee argue, "religion" was primarily understood in the Western conceptual framework that easily turns religion into "a means of identifying persons, places, and societies."[60] Interreligious dialogue including the discipline of religious studies cannot rest on a systematic study of the people and their religions. Green and Searle-Chatterjee contend, that will only "amplify voices at centres of power (whether in Europe or elsewhere) that have attributed or imposed standardisation of practice and belief."[61] Those who are behind the scene remain the power house, and through the use of linguistic terms, their imposed values further strengthen the "representational discourse" on the other.[62] Adherents of other religious traditions will remain a homogenous group to be worked upon.

A Shift of Terminologies in Christian Service: From "the Poor" to "Mission Partner"

In addition to intellectual debate, Christian mission has seen a progressive emphasis on humanitarian aid, relief work and community development. Whereas institutionalized dialogue aims to enlighten the elite leaders, development programs are designed to empower people at the grassroots level.

Early in the Uppsala Assembly (1968), the WCC declared that "the world's agenda" is "the church's business." The Fourth Assembly, as Victor E. W. Hayward predicted, was "more world-oriented than any of the earlier Assemblies."[63] That immediately associated the subject of Christian mission with serving suffering humanity. Since the 1960s, the concept of God's mission has been tied to serving in contexts where socio-economic injustices were rampant. Later, the theme of the Nairobi Assembly (1975),

60. Vatican, "Pontifical Council for Interreligious Dialogue."
61. Green and Searle-Chatterjee, *Religion, Language, and Power*, 2–3.
62. Green and Searle-Chatterjee, *Religion, Language, and Power*, 2–3.
63. Hayward, "World Council's Fourth Assembly," 48.

"Confessing Christ Today," connected evangelism with social agenda. A report of the meeting reads,

> The gospel includes: the announcement of God's kingdom and love through Jesus Christ, the offer of grace and forgiveness of sins, the invitation to repentance and faith in him, the summons to fellowship in God's church, the command to witness to God's saving words and deeds, the responsibility to participate in the struggle for justice and human dignity, the obligation to denounce all that hinders human wholeness, and a commitment to risk life itself.[64]

The word, "social agenda," or "social development" was gradually replaced by a much broader category of transformation. One fundamental question that guides the Commission on World Mission and Evangelism (CWME) of the WCC on drafting its new mission statement for the Busan Assembly (2013) reads,

> Life in the Holy Spirit is the essence of mission, the core of why we do what we do, and how we live our lives. Spirituality gives deepest meaning to our lives and motivates our actions. It is a sacred gift from the Creator, the energy for affirming and caring for life. This mission spirituality has a dynamic of transformation which, through spiritual commitment of people, is capable of transforming the world in God's grace. How can we reclaim mission as transformative spirituality which is life-affirming?[65]

The focus on transformation and its related cognates, such as life-affirming and caring for life, are now widely accepted as the objectives of mission and evangelism. The concept of world-oriented mission or transformation has found a variety of expressions, including ending hunger, eliminating poverty, fighting injustices, living with dignity, and the list goes on.

Transformation Is Given to the Poor

While Christian service is becoming a popular strategy for Christian mission, it is important to point out the hidden agenda behind it. Perhaps it is not so much a hidden agenda as an open secret. The precondition for receiving aid and assistance is to register the person with the label of "poor"

---

64. Nairobi Assembly report quoted in Ott, Strauss, and Tennent, *Encountering Theology of Mission*, 131–32.

65. Keum, "Introduction to the New WCC Mission Statement," 294.

who by no means can survive or thrive without help and support. In some cases, Christian organizations in non-Western countries do not work with anyone who is poor, but only those who are "the poorest of the poor." A lot of paper works needs to be done to identify and to prove whether one is really in need. Despite all the frustrating procedures, "walking with the poor" comes to be a household name in the area of Christian development. Among those who advocate equal relationship between giver and receiver, I want to focus on Bryant L. Myers's concept of transformative development. Based on his years of experience working with World Vision International, Myers believed the effectiveness of Christian relief and development work is highly dependent on the transformation of an individual and thus the person's wider community. In other words, a Christian developer does not work alone and he or she will walk together with the poor. Myers preferred the term "transformational development" which is "seeking positive change in the whole of human life materially, socially, psychologically and spiritually. . . . Transformation implies changing our choices."[66] Transformation signifies a change from the inside out. Any change in a community is dependent on the change in an individual person's life. That change is not limited to the behavioral level, but the entirety of a person, including the person's mindset and ethical system. This kind of holistic change makes growth at both the individual and societal levels sustainable because the person will learn to stand on his or her own feet.

Christians and missionaries involved with the helping profession are highly praised for their dedication and good intentions. There are however ambivalent attitudes to missionary work with good intentions. "To hell with good intentions," Ivan Illich remarked, sternly.[67] "This is a theological statement," as he continues.[68] Illich, best known for his polemical writings against Western institutions, made clear that no intention is good if one's messiah complex is not dealt with properly. Illich called any unreflective helping mentality "hypocrisy."[69]

66. Myers, *Walking With the Poor*.

67. Ivan Illich, founder of the Centro Intercultural de Documentación (CIDOC) at Cuernavaca in Mexico, a research center offering courses for missionaries from North America, was best known for his polemical writings against western institutions and systems. Illich openly criticized the ideology of paternalism when delivering his address to Conference on InterAmerican Student Projects in Cuernavaca. Illich, "To Hell with Good Intentions."

68. Illich owed his theological insight to the Irish saying that goes "the road to hell is paved with good intentions."

69. Illich considered the well-off American students who came to "help" poor Mexicans in the late 1960s were only enjoying "mission-vacations" across the border. These students failed the people of their own context, for their benevolent acts were never

Indeed, the relationship between missionary and the indigenous was predominantly expressed in terms of colonial activity over the past few centuries. Accusations of ethnocentrism and cultural imposition have tainted the reputation of the Christian missionary movement. Church leaders, missiologists, and ecumenists have since held regular meetings to discuss ways to make Christian mission more relevant than it has been in the past. These efforts of making a difference tend to focus on the matter of how. How do we make missionary work better? How do we come to know better the targets of evangelism and to make converts easier? How do we help those less fortunate around the world? The ultimate aim of these questions is not descriptive but prescriptive.

When help is preferably given to the poor abroad but not the poor at home, it really prompts us to interrogate the help or the helping mentality involved in missionary work. Does it mean missionary work is developed exclusively for them (people out there) and not for us (people in here)? It appears that mission discourses that are problem-based largely operate on a scarcity model. The other side is lacking, so the other is constantly required to meet the (hidden) standards. International mission conferences are convened to empower the other. Insights and suggestions from these conferences will not be applicable to the missionary's place of birth. It reminds me of the saying that goes "teaching people to fish and not giving them the fish." It gets popularized in order to avoid creating the dependency syndrome among the recipients. But what happens when all the fish are gone to sustain the consumerist culture in the West? Whose problem is that? The spatial rift between local and global reveals the self-centeredness deposited in mission discourses. Self-centric intents function in a reality in which Christian mission is predicated on the problematic other.

Furthermore, when "global concerns" outweigh "local needs," defining what is mission and what is not becomes even more ambiguous. Whereas working with people overseas is called mission, working with people in local context is named urban ministry or social ministries. Ethnic conflict in non-Western regions is phrased peace and reconciliation in the agenda of global mission, but similar cases are understood as racism and social justice in western societies. Whose interests will be served when we allow the ambiguous definitions of Christian transformative mission programs to go unchallenged? What can we say to those who are committed to ethnic conflict and peace-building projects abroad while remaining silent to racial injustice at home? The problem of the helping mentality that comes along

---

materialized to the life of the suffering and poor in their own backyard. Illich, "To Hell with Good Intentions."

with Christian mission is not simply about having double standards, but the fear of losing power in the global world.

That is why Illich's polemical writings, however insightful, did not stop the influx of missionary activities and service trips to the less developed contexts. There is even a rise in the trend of sending short-termers, especially young men and women, overseas to do mission work. In fact, Christian involvement in service ministries overseas is not new. What needs our attention is the continuation of transmitting Western political values and economic structures to the less developed regions through global service ministry. Joerg Rieger argued we have to place the enthusiasm of Christian service within the framework of imperialist mentality. Rieger observes,

> In the high imperial era after the 1880s, missionary enterprises were still in full swing. At this time, the North American missions had taken the lead in global missions, modeling an activist and pragmatic spirit. People simply wanted to help those in other parts of the world who seemed less fortunate. . . . Here, power was once again supported politically, yet now with an increasing emphasis on economic structures. Once again, the power differential between colonizers and colonized was perceived as an authority differential. No wonder that this approach saw mission basically as a one-way street, moving from the wealthy to the poor or, in terms that probably reflect better the mindset of those who were trying to help, moving from the "civilized" to the "primitives," or from the "more developed" to the "less developed."[70]

I do not say that helping others is wrong, but a reinforcement of the imperialist mentality can be damaging. We have seen the tendency of Christian organizations to institutionalize capacity building programs at the grassroots level. The concept of empowerment aims to help the poor and marginalized to gain control over their lives through education, such as human rights training and entrepreneurial practice. The programs are clothed in new languages, but their contents continue to follow along the values of Western democracy. When these new terminologies are so foreign to local people, their inability to grasp the meaning of that makes them more vulnerable and susceptible to imported ideas for life-changing opportunities.

70. Rieger, "Theology and Mission," 204.

A New Paradox: The Poor Become Partners in Mission

Another subtle form of transmitting Western thinking and cultural ideals is found in the language of partnership. In the post-colonial era, many mainline churches in the Global North have popularized the term "global mission partners" as they seek ways to continue missionary work worldwide. The indigenous people are strategically upgraded to become local partners in God's mission.

Jonathan Barnes unashamedly claims that the history of international partnerships is "fraught with relationships of paternalism, control, and hierarchy as well."[71] The problem of partnership ironically originated from the term itself. Lothar Bauerochse, in *Learning to Live Together: Interchurch Partnerships as Ecumenical Communities of Learning*, claims that

> the term partnership is a term of the colonial era. . . . It is a formula of the former "rulers," who with it wished to both signal a relinquishment of power and also to secure their influence in the future. Therefore, the term can also serve both in colonial policy and mission policy to justify continuing rights of the white minority.[72]

While securing the ruler's influence in the future provides the primary motivation for the ruler to work with the people, that kind of relationships is characterized by goal, productivity and efficiency. Partnership comes with certain kinds of contractual obligations. When uncritically applying this term to missionary activities, mission agencies and societies require the locals to be accountable. Not only do the relationships between one another become functional and mechanical, but the mechanism of partnership makes the people overly reliant on Western know-how and skill sets. To abide by the spirit of partnership means that the locals are expected to speak and act like their Western counterparts.

The nature of ecumenical partnerships can never be equal, given the fact that resources are unevenly distributed across the world. Barnes believes it is naïve to think that paternalistic thinking and practices are a thing of the past. Barnes asserts, "Today, recognizing the inequalities in our world necessitates that those engaged in partnerships not do so uncritically but with intentionally in seeking relationships that subvert and challenge power asymmetries."[73]

---

71. Barnes, "Ambivalence of Partnership," 28.

72. Bauerochse quoted in Barnes, "Ambivalence of Partnership," 29–30.

73. Barnes, "Ambivalence of Partnership," 30.

Challenging power asymmetries means challenging the imperialist thinking embedded in the practice of partnership. The indigenous are wise enough to do things on their own, without necessarily relying on the supervision of the missionary. To take that discourse to another level, good deeds alone are inadequate to assure full personhood of the other in the so-called mission field. Recipients or receivers of good work habitually remain a group of people being accompanied and made to be accountable to the accompaniers. We need to assure the individuality and agency of a person not be compromised in the mission programs that determines what is a success story.

Mission societies and agencies have long dictated the use of terms and precisely the discourse of Christian mission. They can also tell us how mission discourses, in particular, the use of specific terms, change over time. Many Christians have witnessed the shift of terminologies and how words that carry racist and sexist overtones have been replaced by more inclusive ones. Abandoning the use of certain words may help change the outlook of the entire mission enterprise from being paternalistic to being sympathetic. But the reality of Christian mission continues to be constructed by those who have access to information and wealth. When the locals express doubts or dissonant views on a specific issue raised by their Western counterparts, they are at best corrected and at worst considered incompetent. Therefore the same narrative goes: These people of the third world share the background of abject poverty in association with rampant corruption and escalating violence in human rights. They are in need of "a lift": economic, political, and/or theological. Adding a few more aid programs to the list of missionary work or simply extending the scope of mission does not answer sufficiently the recurrent issue of agency in the Christian missionary movement. The indigenous are actively participating in the task of re-shaping missiological orientation. They seek to keep the initiative going. This has both practical and psychological influences. No identity should be received in its pure passivity. We fail the people whom we serve, when we (mis)lead them to aspire to Western cultural values and ideals. Any new missiological term that rationalizes self-gratification empties the meaning of it.

Summary

By probing into the history of Christian missionary movement, I demonstrated how the relations and tensions between missionary and the indigenous have been regulated through mission discourses. The shift of terminologies in the areas of interreligious engagement and Christian service clearly indicated that otherness is more than an imagined concept, but it is something that is subjected to the missioner's scrutinization and interpretation. The gathering of facts and data about the other, and eventually the presentation of that, can be crafty. Categorizing the other becomes even more arbitrary when it is based on biased information. Mission discourses that infuse the binarial relations of self and other into daily operations become particularly appealing. It is such discourses that create the urgency for the task of soul saving. They can also provide an easy access that satisfies the craving of feel-goodism, and eventually, validate self-fulfilling prophecies.

Conceptualizing missiological ideas in a single linguistic system is undesirable and also harmful. Not only will it preserve bias in self against the other, but linguistic inequality also prevents one from recognizing the value of the other. There is an incessant concern about misconstruing the indigenous and their cultures. As early as the 1910 Edinburgh Conference, V. S. Azariah, a young Indian representative, spoke against the paternalistic approach of Western mission. He says, "You have given your goods to feed the poor. You have given your bodies to be burned. We also ask for *love*. Give us FRIENDS!"[74] His famous speech was so powerful that it put the egotistic tendencies of missionary work to shame. Azariah's insight is still relevant in today's world. When we prize progress over self-examination, the solution offered does not really address the core of the issue. The power differentials embedded in the mission discourses remain unchallenged. All vision statements of opening a space of mutuality and promoting diversity remain empty talk, if difference is not engaged, sincerely. Regulating the agenda of Christian mission will fuel the narrative that the missioner is attempting to rattle the sense of self that belongs to the other. Other will only reside in the time and space pre-determined by the missioner-self.

Christian mission involves a constant process of reflection and repentance before we can talk about rejoicing in the wonders of God. The task of reflection does not aim to shame anyone or inflict guilt, or intensify the self-other binary by encouraging anti-West sentiments, but to turn compromises and dilemmas into a source of inspiration. It is necessary to recognize the pain of certain communities, and to honor and embrace their memories as part of the history of Christianity. Taking seriously a multiplicity of voices in the entire mission enterprise is important. It will lead us to rethink the ontological and epistemological distinction between self and other, and in the meantime, the reflection opens new avenues to radicalize language and practice in missionary activities.

74. Azariah quoted in Stanley, *World Missionary Conference*, 125.

4

Confronting Self-Centrism in the Christian Missionary Movement

RE-SHAPING CHRISTIAN MISSION BEGINS with a critical reflection on self. To confront self-centrism in Christian missionary movement, I will first explain how self perceives oneself differently to other individuals. Then I will argue why the process of de-centering self is indispensable for the wellbeing of the other. Attending to the aspect of relationality will broaden our horizons with a renewed sense of self, other, and the world. The interrelatedness of self and other should lead to a whole new level of human solidarity, which further ushers in a new direction for missiological exploration.

A Crisis in Epistemology: Self-Absolutization and De-humanization of the Other

Self and the Civilizing Mission

Achieving self-actualization and boosting one's self-confidence are increasingly compelling in our time. In regard to the Western conception of personhood, Clifford Geertz observes,

> The Western conception of the person as a bounded, unique, more or less integrated motivational and cognitive universe, the dynamic center of awareness, emotion, judgment, and action organized into a distinctive whole and set contrastively both against other such wholes and against its social and natural background is, however incorrigible it may seem to us, a rather peculiar idea within the context of the world's cultures. Rather than attempting to place the experience of others within the framework of such a conception, which is what the extolled

"empathy" in fact usually comes down to, understanding them demands setting that conception aside and seeing their experiences within the framework of their own idea of what selfhood is.[1]

The belief that the Western self is more superior to the non-Western other is nothing new. What Geertz exposes is how Western domination perpetuates itself by subjugating non-Western cultures and reading them into the Western epistemological framework. Only the knowledge of the West carries universal significance, and the experience of the other becomes secondary. The knowing self embodies the ability to think, speak, and act. The other is to play a catch-up game. Thus J. Kameron Carter criticizes, as soon as Western civilization sees itself the center of focus, the world is divided into "the West and the rest."[2] The horizons of the Western world do not stop impacting (and in some extreme cases, colliding with) the culture of other worlds.

In view of the modern form of colonialism, Ashis Nandy asserts the implicit form of Westernization operates almost entirely on an unconscious level for it does "produce not merely models of conformity but also models of 'official' dissent . . . Even when in opposition, that dissent remains predictable and controlled."[3] Using code words is a common rhetorical and linguistic tactic to repress the voices of other and finally, to silence them. Hijacking positive vocabulary means denying the people access to the vocabulary that expresses their emotions and statements. While modern imperialists continue to regulate the speech of the other, they absolutize the system of knowledge and expectations that further dictates the discourse on otherness.

The making and re-making of other rest upon the moral authority of self. Generally speaking, justifying one's moral standards enables one to shame and stigmatize other. In the case that Nandy presents, one can idealize the other. The idealization turns the other to act like self, so that self may love the other. That love is ironically the subjective sense of feeling safe. The creation of the other also makes the self in which self feels greater than other. The making of self necessitates an imposition of values and restrictions over a certain group of people and their activities for the sake of maintaining one's privilege in the larger society.

1. Geertz, *Local Knowledge*, 59.

2. J. Kameron Carter, "On 'the Global' in Global Civil Society: Towards a Theological Archaeology of the Present," in Storrar, Casarella, and Metzger, *World for All?*, 300.

3. Nandy, *Intimate Enemy*, xii.

When Christian mission is understood within the arbitrariness of a particular linguistic framework, the ensuing conception inherits a certain form of epistemology that validates a certain perspective but denies the other, and defends the interests of a certain group but ignores the other. For instance, in critiquing the formation of the American self, Philip Cushman points out, "We all tell historical stories, and by doing so we all take certain moral positions . . . in order to create, shape, and maintain a particular historical self, that all of these selves have had important political and economic functions within their eras."[4] By developing some kind of origin myths about the work that a particular group of people is doing in a particular geographical area, that particular group can build authority over the other, and justify any forms of aggressive acts in the territory.[5]

Cushman's argument clearly illustrates that self is a construct. The emergence of a self-concept is linked with the person's social location. Factors such as economic status, education, gender and citizenship can affect how one perceives oneself (and the other) in the world. The Western self has evolved around the concept of civilization. According to Pieter Vos & Onno Zijlstra, "the concept of civilization goes back to eighteenth-century thinkers who developed the idea of civilization as the opposite of barbarism."[6] That specific term was invented to separate those who practiced and pursued higher standards of morality from those who did not.[7] Vos & Zijlstra explain how Western civilization becomes the model for other cultures: European leaders and thinkers have endorsed the use of a set of standards to evaluate non-European societies, and the difference turned out to be a degree of civility. The subjective assessment of who is more 'civilized' and who is not becomes "now objectified."[8] Vos & Zijlstra continue, civilization is "defined in terms of *results* rather than processes."[9]

As soon as civilization was understood in terms of results, it impacted the orientation of missionary activities. Vos & Zijlstra do not deny responsibility of scholars and church leaders who relate Christianity to an expansion of Western civilization. Vos & Zijlstra observe, "Western people saw their own civilization as better and more civilized than other civilizations. The world had to be civilized in the direction of Western Christian

---

4. Cushman, *Constructing the Self*, 35.

5. Cushman, *Constructing the Self*, 35.

6. Vos and Zijlstra, *Law of God*, 2.

7. Vos and Zijlstra, *Law of God*, 2.

8. Vos and Zijlstra, *Law of God*, 3.

9. Vos and Zijlstra, *Law of God*, 3.

civilizations."[10] The identification of "we" as gospel-bearers as opposed to "they" as gospel-receivers becomes normative for the purpose of differentiation. The building of a positive self-image for Western Christianity is actually predicated upon the backwardness of the other. The knowing self has the final say on the other's social life, political choices, economic activities, and even religious matters.

It should be noted that similar criticism of the intermingling of Christianity and Western civilization is available intermittently. Missiologists and theologians, such as David Bosch and Lesslie Newbigin, spoke against the legacies of the Enlightenment. Bosch is cautious about the bias and prejudice deposited in Western cultural values, and says that the spread of Western Christianity will inevitably perpetuate white privilege.[11] In the lectures that Newbigin delivered at the United Theological College in Bangalore in 1947, he challenged the conviction that Europeans were the born leaders of the world. Western civilization with the very idea of progress brought harmful effects to the languages, cultures and thought-forms of people of other races. To Newbigin, the idea of progress is dangerous, as it usurps the sovereignty of God through exalting humanity's virtue and reasoning power.[12]

Even Paul Hiebert, anthropologist, unashamedly criticized the sense of superiority ingrained in Western epistemology. The practice of dichotomizing cultures and people holds particular salience in the so-called mission fields. While missionaries advanced the gospel to the land of heathens in the name of civilizing mission, they failed to challenge the ideology of imperialism and recognize adverse effects of their own worldviews on the indigenous culture. Hiebert critiques, "Why do we demand radical changes and great sacrifices of new converts when in our homelands Christianity is largely captive to our cultural and social systems?"[13] He warned us that our epistemological stances directly affect how we understand the gospel, how we view others and how we treat them.[14] Thus Hiebert conceptualized the

10. Vos and Zijlstra, *Law of God*, 3.

11. Bosch believed Christians of the twentieth century witnessed the most important moments in the history of Christian mission. It was the time when Christians expanded their consciousness to the impact of the Enlightenment. The Enlightenment's emphasis on human reasoning distorted the basis and nature of Christian mission. Therefore Bosch asserted that the foundation of mission is not built on human rationality, but on the self-definition of Jesus, whose teaching consistently challenged the attitudes of his disciples and their acts of building walls and drawing boundaries between one another. Bosch, *Transforming Mission*.

12. Newbigin, *Signs amid the Rubble*, 4–6.

13. Hiebert, *Missiological Implications of Epistemological Shifts*, xiv.

14. Hiebert, *Anthropological Reflections on Missiological Issues*, 45

relational problem as one of epistemological "crisis" leading the West to the quest for global dominance.[15] He also believed the objectification of the other effectually became the breeding ground for modern racism.[16]

These efforts of exposing the hypocrisy in Western-centric missionary movement, however, did not immediately eliminate the multi-layered hierarchy in Christian mission. Despite a new focus on friendship building, there are complaints of the existence of missionaries who still forcibly convert people of other religions. People of color often feel isolated in predominantly white mission boards and associations.

Self-Centric Mission in the Age of Individualism

The task of de-centering self is ineffective because the sense of self has become individualized and so internalized. The need to be seen as useful underscores a self-centered missiology. A self-centered narrative can develop into an implicit form of respectability that requires others to appreciate the work done to them. Hessel Zondag clearly points out that the desire of gaining recognition displays a major symptom of narcissism. Zondag writes,

> Narcissistic people are constantly on the lookout for recognition and reassurance. They need other people's admiration to confirm their imagined greatness. A lack of admiration from others results in feelings of emptiness, depletion, apathy, and a sense of not really living. It is precisely these feelings which constitute the core of narcissistic vulnerability.[17]

Nell Ziehl, who has years of experience dealing with narcissistic personality disorder (NPD), shares her observation of how a person with NPD speaks and acts. She referenced the speech and behaviors of the current president of the United States, Donald Trump. I will not go through every point Ziehl listed, but I want to highlight the danger of caring about oneself and those closest and most beloved. It means that, in Ziehl's words, "People with NPD often can't understand others as fully human or distinct."[18] Now I am not saying all missionaries are narcissistic. When missionaries come from a culture that indicates high levels of narcissism, how can we ensure that their worldviews and language are not impacted by their culture? We all know the danger of not doing anything to resist unjustifiable circumstances,

15. Hiebert, *Anthropological Reflections on Missiological Issues*, 20.
16. Hiebert, *Gospel in Human Contexts*, 68.
17. Zondag, "Just Like Other People," 424.
18. Ziehl, "Coping with Narcissistic Personality Disorder."

because it can enable that kind of culture to thrive. Missionaries need to honestly deal with the problems of their culture or narcissistic tendencies, if they want to prove that they respect others and their cultures.

Self-promoting strategies intensify the messiah-complex of the missioner, and the accompanying story limits the possibility of mission thinking and practice. It is commonplace to hear discourses such as 'we are here to help,' 'we are here for a cause,' 'we want to protect the people,' 'we want to change lives' and so forth. I do not deny the value of serving ministries or diakonia in general. What I oppose, instead, is the expectation of changing other people and their social systems without intending to change oneself and adjust one's cultural values. The kind of practice that focuses on helping the other yet disrespects the other's perspectives and feelings is self-centered. Wanting to gain recognition becomes the driving force, because of its emotional and psychological impact on those who deliver help and service to the other; meanwhile, it can be once more exercising power over the other. When one does something to the other truly out of good conscience, one does not expect anything in return or magnify the work done to the other. People will appreciate it and express gratitude in their own way. This is how we tell the story, but not impose our agenda on the others.

Charles Taylor rightly observed that modern individualism presumed each individual as autonomous and the sovereignty of individuals easily gave birth to a culture of authenticity.[19] Such a culture "encourages a purely personal understanding of self-fulfillment, thus making the various association and communities in which the person enters purely instrumental in their significance."[20] Being authentic is being good; gaining recognition is a prerequisite for success. Therefore, the primary function of relationship is to fulfill the interests of self.[21] As interpersonal relationships become "secondary" to the project of self-realization, Taylor concludes, "Authenticity seems once more to be defined here in a way that centers on the self, which distances us from our relations to others."[22] When the need to succeed takes center stage in Christian mission, the unchecked desire will lead one to pursue fame and power. That further distract one from what is more significant.

The individualistic understanding of self is devoid of a communal sense. Self neither carries a connotation of a "we" nor functions as a community of selves. Self refers to an "I" that forms a boundary and separates "I" from my neighbor. Christian mission becomes a platform for expressing

19. Taylor, *Ethics of Authenticity*, 44.
20. Taylor, *Ethics of Authenticity*, 43.
21. Taylor, *Ethics of Authenticity*, 43.
22. Taylor, *Ethics of Authenticity*, 43–44.

and exercising one's individuality. We only fixate on our selves. Thus Mark Freeman, phenomenologist and psychologist, says that "our selves are important to us; so it is that we protest when our selves . . . are denied, negated, or hurt, or when our creativity and freedom are not given room to grow and flourish."[23] Self-absorption obscures our vision of building healthy relationships with the other. In Miroslav Volf's words, self is constructed to exclude.[24] The means of exclusion, including assimilation, domination, abandonment, and elimination, turn us against our neighbors. This kind of self-righteousness keeps us apart from them, and this very practice of exclusion mirrors the sinful nature of humanity. The gap between self and other is widening.

Turning the Table: A De-centered Self

Self is a construct. There is no such thing as a self. The sense of self is a way that helps one to know who one is and thus to make sense of the world. But sometimes, what has been constructed for self through the process of socialization can distort facts about the world in order to create a self that is better than the other. Our notion of self will be changed when we come into contact with the other. Our identities are not static, but multiple and transformable. We need to first empty what has been falsely constructed for self.

Self-Emptying Is Not Denying One's Personhood

The concept of self-emptying becomes relevant and timely to address the issue of egocentrism in Christian missionary movement. In Philippians 2:1–11, Christ Jesus' willingness to "empty himself" in human likeness even to the point of death speaks clearly about God's faithfulness for humanity. To empty himself, Jesus gives up his power and privilege, and resigns himself to the will of God. What does it mean for us to give up our power and privilege while doing missionary work? There is a striking difference between giver and receiver, in terms of material wealth, financial status, and technological know-how. How we resolve the difference is one thing, and how we deal with the power and privilege implied in the difference is quite another. Giving, in particular, financial giving, is a good illustration. Nowadays, missionary work is frequently associated with providing humanitarian aids and services; Jim Harries and Fred Lewis argue that Christian missionary

23. Freeman, *Priority of the Other*, 4–5.
24. Volf, *Exclusion & Embrace*, 30.

activities "translate . . . into one thing—money."[25] Based on their study of how Western Christians impact African cultures, Harries and Lewis criticize that "Western Christians see money as 'help,' but often do not see it as an expression of power . . . our missionary power can unwittingly encourage lying and deception to keep the money coming in."[26]

When money has become the primary means to deliver the good news and to sustain the good work, Christian mission runs the risk of idolizing money. That does not help people understand the good news at all. Mission agencies and societies are required to constantly interrogate various forms of (earthly) powers being involved in missionary activities. Clearly, relationships are neither operated nor motivated by money power. Relationships are mediated by the self-emptying love of Jesus. Jesus has demonstrated the most humble yet powerful way to love what God loves. His abandoning of self-seeking motives manifested through the form of self-giving provides us a model to relate to our neighbors.

Furthermore, Jesus' self-emptying love is given to all people, and "all" means every single human being. There is no difference between self and other, when it comes to the universal love of God in Jesus Christ. It does not say those sinners need it more than we do. We admit that we also are sinners in need of salvation. In a conversation between Pope Francis and the Vatican reporter Andrea Tornielli, Pope Francis was asked "How do we recognize that we ourselves are sinners? What would you say to someone who doesn't feel like one?" He then replies,

> I would advise him to ask for the grace of feeling like one! Yes, because even recognizing oneself as a sinner is a grace. It is a grace that is granted to you. Without that grace, the most one can say is: I am limited, I have my limits, these are my mistakes. But recognizing oneself as a sinner is something else. It means standing in front of God, who is our everything, and presenting him with our selves, which are nothing. Our miseries, our sins. What we need to ask for is truly an act of grace.[27]

Self-emptying is not self-denial. It does not nullify 'who we are,' but 'who we are' is not defined by social norms and even self-fulfilling prophesies. Our true identities are dependent on the grace of God. God's grace is given to us when we are in utmost confusion or when we arrogantly claim that humanity is an active agent of change. Human beings believe that by their own nature they can be good and they tend to assume the role of God.

25. Harries and Lewis, "Is Mission Diverse," 347.

26. Harries and Lewis, "Is Mission Diverse," 353.

27. Francis, *Name of God Is Mercy*, 32.

The grace of God confronts our egotistic self. We are just like the other, broken yet beloved created beings. Self is no better than the other. The grace of God enables us to see that as part of God's creation, we depend not on earthly powers but the life-giving God. The grace of God is the grace embodied in Jesus Christ and it is this grace that gives hope. Precisely David Jenson asserts, "Kenosis offers one shape of hope for the future. To sustain such hope in the midst of suffering, destruction, and the arrogation of self-privilege is but one aspect of the new life that Christians have always proclaimed."[28]

Jesus' self-emptying love on the cross confronts violence of any form; his death and resurrection envision a path of transformation. Being centered in God steers us away from being inward-looking and provides the basis for our way of being that further readies us to live a life for the well-being of others. In the newness of life, we reject violence and injustice being inflicted on the invisible communities. With the resurgence of other world religions, the concept of self-emptying is of paramount importance. David Jenson maintains, "A focus on the kenotic Christ, in short, de-centers the self to make room for others. . . . The time has now come for the articulation of that hope in the company of the religious Other, and to add yet another voice to the distinctive, yet ever changing shape of Christian identity in a pluralistic world."[29] As we open ourselves to different conceptions of personhood, and different concepts of ways of life, we will be humbled by the vast array of stories of other. In the meantime, we offer ourselves an alternative to life.

Self as "Guest"

The notion of self-emptying underscores the importance of humility. Theologians and missiologists try to develop game-changing ideas to resist the hedonistic predispositions. Christians used to be the host to welcome guests and strangers. Through a display of Christian hospitality, Christians hope to demonstrate Christ's love for all people. While the diffusion of Christianity continues to depend on such a Christian-centric model, being hospitable is not a uniquely Christian metaphor. People of the global South are always ready to treat others hospitably, because hospitality is part of their cultures. Kosuke Koyama believes hospitality does not stand alone. It has to be complemented by mutuality and reciprocity. In his speech at the Eighth Assembly of the WCC in Harare, Koyama asserts, "We cannot love our neighbours unless we are open to being loved by our neighbours.

---

28. Jensen, *In the Company of Others*, 186.

29. Jensen, *In the Company of Others*, 186.

We cannot extend hospitality to strangers unless we accept hospitality from strangers."[30]

Christians are both givers and receivers of love. Through practicing and receiving hospitality, Christians will learn to appreciate an analogy for dethroning self from being the host to guest upon missionary encounter. Christians are guests among the other. This holds true in the religiously pluralistic contexts where Christians are set to be a minority. Imagine when Christians invite themselves to a Muslim-majority country, they later invite their Muslim friends or potential evangelism targets to a place they call home. The persons who are guests in the Christian home are expected to show honor to the host. That ambivalent host-guest relation raises the question of who we want to honor in those situations. Missionaries and practitioners are invited to discover the work of God for humanity and the world, along with the missionized.

Felix Ehimare Enegho and Friday John Imekh remind us that missionaries are expected to play by the game and not set the rules of the game. Enegho and Imekh point out, " Going on mission is not a kind of picnic or jamboree; therefore anyone who has offered him or herself as a missionary must be someone who is ready to abide by the rules," such as "when to be persuasive as well as when to make use of the language of compulsion; the reason is that doing the right thing at the wrong time can sometimes be disastrous."[31] Seeing things from the standpoint of a guest enables one to appreciate the wisdom of the other, and helps one to discern the work of God in and through respective communities.

Self as "the Stranger"

Another suggestion puts an emphasis on self as "stranger." This idea is biblically grounded. For example, it is written, "You shall also love the stranger, for you were strangers in the land of Egypt" (Deuteronomy 10:19). The image of a stranger usually is associated with unpredictability, fear, and even violence. Lisa Isherwood and David Harris find that the perception toward the stranger has long been a hindrance to Christian hospitality. So they flip the table and argue, "The Christian is always, or should always be, the stranger in a strange land, the one who is able to see with different eyes the culture in which he or she lives in order to embody the counter-cultural revolution that the early Jesus movement felt itself to be."[32]

30. Koyama, "Rejoice in Hope," 40.

31. Enegho and Imaekhai, "Language and Christian Evangelism," 346.

32. Isherwood and Harris, *Radical Otherness*, 38.

Isherwood and Harris are not simply talking about the stranger who lives in us. Certainly, we are stranger in the hidden part of our nature, but Isherwood and Harris ask that we remember and embrace this alien identity. As we live as a foreigner, we can experience our vulnerability and because of that, we can see "the very essence of an incarnational Christology: one in which Christ is not a fixed eternal absolute but rather journeys with us as the stranger within, the one who is strange to us and makes us strange to ourselves."[33] We will have the courage to confront our aggression and intolerance of the other.

I find the observation of Isherwood and Harris particularly helpful when juxtaposed with a Zen saying, known as *Mountains are Mountains*.

> I saw mountains as mountains, and waters as waters. When I arrived at a more intimate knowledge, I came to the point where I saw that mountains are not mountains, and waters are not waters. But now that I have got its very substance I am at rest. For it's just that I see mountains once again as mountains, and waters once again as waters.[34]

Self as a stranger asks us to unlearn what is familiar in our theological orientation. Preconceived ideas tend to lead us to prioritize results over the process. We thought we got it, but we did not. We thought we knew the answer, but we did not. We reach a point of desperation when our knowledge fails to explain the unfamiliarity of the world. Uncertainty and uneasiness abound. Truth does not rest upon our rationality. Light comes through the tunnel only when we depend on nothing but the grace of God, solely and absolutely. I do not want to repeat what I mentioned earlier about the grace of God, but I want to emphasize that the grace of God is the source of enlightenment and the frame of reference to begin with. When we abandon our preconceived ideas, we are able to see.

To be a stranger will also free us from being attached to the desires of getting attention and feeling useful. It helps us avoid the temptation to privatize missionary work and make past achievement equivalent to our true selves. We are not defined by success and productivity; lest we are indulging in the fruit of our own effort, which easily falls prey to the trap of unlimited pursuit of fame and power. Narcissism is hard to see in ourselves. We need to be aware of our self-views and impulsive tendencies. Otherwise, we end up controlling the form of practice but are uninterested in the content of missionary engagement. Being a stranger is therefore more about

---

33. Isherwood and Harris, *Radical Otherness*, 38.
34. Watts, *Way of Zen*, 126.

believing and living in the good. We set ourselves on a journey to build relationships with the other and to learn to respect their values and wisdom.

Reconstructing Self: A Pathway to Human Flourishing

A Call for Interdependence and Interconnectedness

Self has to be placed within the framework of relationality. Its communal sense inevitably outweighs an expression of individuality. Reconstructing self alludes to a call for interdependence and interconnectedness. One appropriate illustration is the concept of 'Ubuntu.' It is widely known as a way of life in Africa. Ubuntu simply translates 'I am because we are.' The intimate relationships between one another are not driven by the principle of survival, but one that emphasizes unity. The significance of the other and the full potential of an individual are intrinsically connected. Because of the other, I can be a human.

A similar concept of interrelationality is found in the Confucius teaching. According to *The Analects* 6:30,

> Tsz-Kung asks about the meaning of humanity (*ren*) and The Master replies, "For a person practicing the virtue of humanity is one who wishes oneself to be established, seeks also to establish others, and, one who wishes oneself to be successful, helps also the others to become successful. To be able to take one's feeling and experience as a guide while relating to the other achieves the art of *ren*." (My translation)

Even the character of *ren* is composed of two people, which carries the meaning of a human being together with other human beings. When one sees another as a human being, it makes a whole lot of difference concerning the topic of relationship. There is goodness, benevolence, and mutual respect between one another. The identity of each individual is derived from constant interactions with other individuals of the broader community. When one practices *ren* and treats the other with goodness, kindness, benevolence, and thoughtfulness, one becomes the *junzi* (a virtuous person). The realization of *ren* epitomizes what it means to be a human being or the ideal of a human being, which consequently persuades others to do likewise.

An Ethical Response to the Other

The concept of interrelationality highlights not only mutual trust and enrichment, but also the wellbeing of the other. The wellbeing of the other is not an added value. It is not something that the Christian community can either opt for or opt out. Being church is being with the other and for the other. Emmanuel Levinas's analysis on the intertwined relationships between self and other will give us some pointers on one's responsibility for others. Levinas considers the encounter with the other totally ethical.[35] Self cannot be understood in isolation. Self and other are inseparable. As Levinas says, self and other are "bound in a knot."[36] Furthermore, self does not exist for one-self. Self bears the responsibility for the other to the point that self is compelled to stand by the other. Levinas insists that self is "devoted to others, without being able to resign, and thus incarnated in order to offer itself, to suffer and to give. It is thus one and unique, in passivity from the start, having nothing at its disposal that would enable it not to yield to provocation."[37] The fact that self is held hostage by the other is unexplainable and incomprehensible. In *Totality and Infinity*, Levinas states, "The strangeness of the Other, his irreducibility to the I, to my thoughts and my possessions, is precisely accomplished as a calling into question my spontaneity as ethics."[38] That is why Levinas believes that self-other relationships are not ontological, but ethical.

Levinas made a special remark on the face of the other. He believes that the face of the other is "too weak," "less than a phenomenon," "nonform," "ageing," "dying," "poverty," and so on.[39] While exposing the nudity of the face of the other, Levinas insists that the other is irreducible.

To summarize Levinas's theory of the alterity, Byungohk Lee writes, "As long as the other cannot be "I," the face of the other naturally leads us into the absolute openness of the Infinite or God. In this light, God continues to speak to us in the face of the other, such as the poor, the stranger, the widow, and the orphan, although God always maintains transcendence."[40] The face of the other forces the self to have an ethical obligation to the other beyond rationality. That encounter transforms the self from inside out, into a new reality of time and space. Levinas asserts that "one-for-the-other has

---

35. Levinas, *Otherwise Than Being*, 102.

36. Levinas, *Otherwise Than Being*, 105.

37. Levinas, *Otherwise Than Being*, 105.

38. Levinas, *Totality and Infinity*, 43.

39. Levinas, *Otherwise Than Being*, 88.

40. Lee, *Missional Hermeneutic of the Other*, 421.

the form of sensibility or vulnerability, pure passivity or susceptivity, passive to the point of becoming an aspiration."[41]

Though appreciating Levinas's contribution to the theory of the other, Lee believes Levinasian ethics focuses too much on the subject of transcendence. Comparing with Confucianism's notion of the other, Lee highlights the significance of self-cultivation not only to the broader community but also to rightly respond to the mandate of Heaven. Thus Lee critiques Levinas's failure to consider the "immanence of the Infinite in the self."[42] Lee continues, "Levinas's emphasis on the other might strengthen the insurmountable differences between the church and the world as the other, thus preventing them from having a dialogue. The more the church emphasizes its responsibility for the other, the less attention it may pay to the other as its interlocutor."[43]

I am not trying to take sides as to decide whether I support Levinas's argument or reject it. There are indeed different ways of human flourishing in various cultural contexts. But I believe emphasizing responsibility in a culture that speaks of individualism is really appropriate and prophetic. Levinas's exposition on the face of the other including the other's nakedness unveils the acuteness of asymmetrical relationships between self and other. When there is a lack of responsibility for the wellbeing of the other, our presupposition of self as a morally autonomous being that meaningfully interacts with other beings in accordance with the Divine will becomes questionable. Levinas's notion of alterity problematizes the arrogant self. This is a wake-up call for those who exhibit self-centric thoughts and behaviors. Levinas has done a good job in bringing back the long lost human virtue.

To demonstrate how being responsible for the other is intrinsic to one's nature, let me quote from the teaching of Mencius. In *Mencius* 2A6, Mencius says,

> Supposing people see a child fall into a well—they all have a heart-mind that is shocked and sympathetic. It is not for the sake of being on good terms with the child's parents, and it is not for the sake of winning praise from neighbors and friends, nor is it because they dislike the child's noisy cry.

> Judging by this, without a heart-mind that sympathizes, one is not human; without a heart-mind aware of shame, one is not human; without a heart-mind that defers to others, one is not

41. Levinas, *Otherwise Than Being*, 67.

42. Lee, *Missional Hermeneutic of the Other*, 421–24.

43. Lee, *Missional Hermeneutic of the Other*, 421.

human; and without a heart-mind that approves and condemns, one is not human.[44]

The feelings of sympathy are highlighted in the analogy. It is also akin to what the parable of the Good Samaritan in Luke 10:33, describes: the person who feels compassion and helps the man who is half-dead on the road. The Greek term for feeling compassion can be understood in English as "gut feeling." To-be-for-the-other necessitates a heart-mind. One cannot separate the heart from the mind, and vice versa. You know what to do and you do what you can, when you see another person is in danger or suffering. This heart-mind also pertains to the interconnectedness of transcendence and immanence of the Way. When one centers his or her mind on the Way, the person will know what is good and bad. The Way dwells in the person. The indwelling of the Way is the realized consciousness that further leads the person to engage human goodness for the wellbeing of the other. (I will explain more in detail in the following chapter). In a similar vein, when Levinas speaks about the face of the other—however ugly and unappetizing—he insists that the other can never be reduced to any form of representations. That irreducibility goes beyond human comprehension. Humanity's inability to explain the being of the other makes the other inviolable. Somehow, Levinas is also convinced that God speaks through the other. Because of that, the very encounter of the other challenges our egotism to the utmost. I am responsible for the other. The surrendering of self including self-serving intents represents a commitment to eradicate hierarchical relationships between one another. This commitment also affirms the interconnectedness of one another, so that I and You can really share and grieve together.

Therefore, the problem is not about being responsible for the other, but how it is understood in specific cultural contexts, and how it is narrated in our missiological discourse. When the greatness of missionary work gets constructed, reported, published, circulated, and reappraised over and again, it is a problem. It is, by no means, an accident. When we are unwilling to look at the face of the other, we are not really interested in the people. We focus only on the work we have done to the other. We overemphasize how we help the other and empower the other. We are trapped in an endless story about vainglory. Our language of excessive vanity only deprives the other of his or her dignity and even personhood. As Mencius reminds us, good work "is not for the sake of winning praise." Instead, it is a way to be human.

44. Cf. Bloom, *Mencius*, 35.

From Responsibility to Human Solidarity

The interrelatedness of self and other leads to a whole new level of human solidarity. According to the Oxford dictionary, solidarity refers to the unity or agreement of feeling or action, especially among individuals with a common interest. Catholic theologian, Gerald Beyer believes, "The conceptual seeds of solidarity lie in the earlier Christian concept of charity" and various Catholic scholars refer to solidarity as "a normative obligation governing interpersonal relations . . . the co-responsibility of each individual for the moral well-being of all others"[45] Making changes is not somebody's responsibility, but all of us. The strengthening of social obligations of individuals and communities for the common good should widen our horizons and imagination and help us explore better ways of working together.

Rebecca Todd Peters's theology of solidarity shows an important shift from focusing on the problems to interrogating the powers in face of tremendous suffering both at home and abroad. Her concept of solidarity emerged from her experiences of helping the poor. It was a moment of (spiritual) awakening for her—which she calls "an experience of *metanoia*"—when she found out that the helping mentality can create unnecessary binaries between the have and the have-not.[46] Peters is not against charity, but she believes we can do more than that. Peters says, candidly that "well-intentioned structures of benevolence and charity inevitably contribute to the creation of imbalanced relationships. These relationships allow first-world Christians to feel good about ourselves."[47]

Focusing too much on the problem of other cultures without re-evaluating those in one's own culture makes one hypocritical. Peters is saying that we should go beyond feeling compassion for the suffering of others, but to strive for justice and equality. See the suffering of the world should force us "to change anything about our own personal habits and behaviors or the social and economic structures that shape our societies in patterns of wealth and poverty, have and have-not, deserving and undeserving."[48] On the one hand, self cannot remain a spectator watching and commenting the flow of events from afar. One has to relate one's environments with the surroundings of the other, if one so desires to partake in the life of the other. On the other hand, Peters considers the other equal. Self and other can work together for the goodness of all.

45. Beyer, "Meaning of Solidarity in Catholic Social Teaching," 13.

46. Peters, *Solidarity Ethics*, xiii.

47. Peters, *Solidarity Ethics*, xiii.

48. Peters, *Solidarity Ethics*, xiii.

Solidarity can be a language that shatters the self-other binary. It obliges us to recognize that the other is subject and not object. These other individuals can point out our weaknesses and lead us to deal with our own problems. Peters asks, "Why are the products at Walmart so cheap? What is that environmental impact of the food that I buy? Why is it that we have so much and our lives are so comfortable when one-third of the world, or 2.4 billion people, live in poverty?"[49] Peters specifically mentioned the way people in the first world live and acquire wealth can have dire consequences for those in the third world. She thus takes it a step further to suggest that those who have power and wealth "come to terms with their own privilege."[50] The purpose of that is not to inflict guilt feelings upon the powerful and the haves, but "to establish God's vision of right relation and justice in the world."[51] How can we do that? Peters suggests that we need to return to "the good news of the gospel," which is not only for them but also for us. As receivers of "God's unending grace," we are forgiven and that liberating message will guide us to build a human community that aspires to friendship, empathy, justice and equality.[52]

Peters makes clear that she does not have all the answers to human suffering and she says, "We need to figure out how to link churches and church communities in the global North and the global South in meaningful ties that are not built on colonialism, paternalism, or resource transfer but that allow real bonds of Christian love and solidarity to be forged together."[53] I think this is an important reminder: None of us is called to save the world. It is not about what we do, but what God does and has done for the sake of the world. "We" together with others are witnesses to God's wondrous deeds for the world. In Christ, we are freed from our messiah complex. We do not take pride in our unrealistic expectations of missionary work; yet, we are freed to be each other's keeper, journeying with others to seek common good.

Summary

I have demonstrated how the formation of self-image changes upon coming into contact with the different other. The quest for identity requires us to be honest about our need for power and control. Emptying self desires is

49. Peters, *Solidarity Ethics*, xiii.

50. Peters, *Solidarity Ethics*, xiii.

51. Peters, *Solidarity Ethics*, 81.

52. Peters, *Solidarity Ethics*, 81; 100.

53. Peters, *Solidarity Ethics*, 109.

necessary for the wellbeing of the other. The renewed sense of self, on the one hand, invites us to greater intimacy with God. Accepting our limitations leads us back to God's faithfulness, mercy and love.

On the other hand, self-emptying opens new avenues to understanding other and the world. This renewed vision attends to the aspect of relationality as opposed to the biased epistemology that brings harmful effects on people and their cultures. Any attempt to reduce other to a form of representation is unethical. More significantly, "we" and "they" are inextricably linked. The interrelatedness of all life makes everyone a keeper of each other.

5

Other and Otherness Revisited

Subverting the Narrative That Maintains Existing Power Structures

IN THE PREVIOUS CHAPTER, I confronted a self-centered approach to Christian mission. In this chapter, I aim to contest discursive strategies that rationalize the fear of the other and to destabilize efforts of evoking anxiety against the other. I will first recapitulate how the category of the other is constructed and how that becomes a point of reference to denigrate the other. In view of that, I urge to revisit otherness and challenge mission discourses that seek to maintain existing power structures. Based on biblical accounts on difference and language, I argue that we should see otherness as gift. Building on the Pentecostal event, every single one is a gifted individual. Every single one is empowered with the ability to speak, pray, and sing. The multiple voices become a cause to celebrate. Any responsible missiological approach to a community of people cannot lose sight of the value of the people. To pose this idea even more strongly, otherness as gift ought to be an emergent perspective for the task of missiological re-imagination. It should help us envision a responsible discourse that rightly speaks power and justly considers the difference between individuals.

Constructing the Other: Difference as a Reference Point to Denigrate, Despise, and Deny

Elevating the subjectivity of oneself easily downplays that of the other. When evaluating ourselves in terms of how we compare to others, we often end up misinterpreting the other. Stories containing negative perceptions of the other proliferated not just in movies, or documentaries, but now online newsfeeds and tweets. Biased descriptions about the indigenous are also found in mission literature and missionary newsletter. Can we truly know their worldviews, feelings, beliefs and aspirations? What people value most in life can be very different from the vision of the mission enterprise. Their lived experiences are however rendered secondary when conceptualizing missiological discourse. Third world cultures are not on par with the (Western) Christian tradition and their impact is largely limited to the local and not the global. Third world theologians are frequently accused of their syncretistic and relativistic tendencies. Who is the other? Who are the people we serve and evangelize in and along the mission frontiers? We have to confront misconceptions and prejudices against the other.

Before we get into specifics, I want to make clear that the topic of otherness involves the life of the other, so any discussion of that requires additional prudence and solemnity. I do not support any research that focuses exclusively on gaining knowledge about the other. As Paul J. Griffiths puts it, "Christian theologians have always been interested in non-Christian religious communities. . . . In the decades since the final decay of the European colonial empires and the end of Europe's most recent attempts at self-destruction, this interest has flourished, grown and, in some respects, changed."[1]

In reaction to researching purely for pleasure and theorizing purposes, Lisa Isherwood and David Harris regard the egocentric motivation as chasing after "exoticized" subjects.[2] Any act of commoditizing the other can be tantamount to "zookeeping" that is both disrespectful and disappointing.[3] Isherwood and Harris go on to criticize that some researchers will try to "engage in normal conversations" with the subjects and through building personal relationship with them, the researchers are able to "understand" their subjects the same way as they understand their friends.[4] However, the data collected can never help us fully understand the subjects of study. The other is always beyond capture. We cannot explain something that is unexplainable. Even keeping the data for further scientific scrutiny implicates imperialist motives to subjugate certain groups of people. Isherwood and Harris allege that these researchers are simply "unable to distance themselves very far from colonialism, despite some of the good intentions."[5]

---

1. Griffiths, *Christianity through Non-Christian Eyes*, 1–2.

2. Isherwood and Harris, *Radical Otherness*, 5.

3. Young quoted in Isherwood and Harris, *Radical Otherness*, 5.

4. Isherwood and Harris, *Radical Otherness*, 5.

5. Isherwood and Harris, *Radical Otherness*, 5.

In addition, I reject any attempt that reduces the identity of the other to a fixed image and otherness to some kind of qualities particularly for fundraising purposes. Any new mission campaigns that turn the other into certain form of representations are suspicious. The assertion that gaining visibility for the other is built on culturally biased assumptions. Manipulating otherness for selfish ends only impoverishes the other and makes them more vulnerable.

The construction of otherness infiltrates all levels of human society. To explicate that, I want to point to the following example. In *Monolingualism*, Jacques Derrida says,

> "I only have one language; it is not mine."
> Or rather, and better still:
> I am monolingual. My monolingualism dwells, and I call it my dwelling; it feels like one to me, and I remain in it and inhabit it. It inhabits me. The monolingualism in which I draw my very breath is, for me, my element. Not a natural element, not the transparency of the ether, but an absolute habitat. It is impassable, *indisputable*: I cannot challenge it except by testifying to its omnipresence in me.[6]

We are dealing with a condition in which one's human agency can be removed, forcefully and completely. Speaking only the master's language makes Derrida feel desperate. He is not himself in the language he speaks. This troubles him. It robs him of his humanity and dignity. The feeling of inferiority pertains to the fact that he lives in a linguistic world that is foreign to him. He cannot speak his own language, the language he is supposed to speak. That identity crisis emerges out of the polity in which everybody is supposed to speak the one and only language. Language is what makes up a person. While the category of the other is created linguistically to shame those who do not conform to certain norms and values, assimilation and appropriation of otherness become a subtle form of social control. Linguistic hegemony attempts to coerce the other to become less alien. The erasure of otherness is inevitable in the social construction of the other.

Three Models of Making the Other

The category of the other is utterly a social construct. Jonathan Z. Smith identifies three basic models of the other. The first one is the metonymical model that has to do with names. According to Smith, "One group distinguishes

---

6. Derrida, *Monolingualism of the Other*, 1.

itself from another by lifting up some cultural feature, expressed as . . . the use of some unfamiliar cultural object (e.g., "fish-eaters," "garlic-eaters"), the presence of some marked physical feature (e.g., "whites," "blacks"), or the characterization of difference."[7] Names are important, because it gives power to the one who names. More than that, names can help one with differentiation. As the society is getting complex, people need different names to call different things. Differentiation can help people make distinction between cultures, languages, and things, despite the arbitrariness deposited in the nomenclature itself. The big question on the act of naming is always, what language is appropriate to call the other? Do we call them what they call themselves? If not, we are describing the other from our point of view which is most often unrealistic. Precisely, we invent the other in our minds.

Second, it is the model of center and periphery. Understood in geographic terms, the center represents the norm and the standard; whereas, the periphery carries the connotations of deviant and lesser significance. Smith observes that "the latter pattern . . . displays spatial 'otherness' most frequently."[8] Other forms of center-periphery binary include a north-south axis and urban-rural. These various contrastive forms have generated numerous labels. Smith says, "The simple dichotomy of city and outlands was generalized into universal types that have proven to be the longest lived designations for 'others' in native, western vocabulary: 'Pagan' . . . 'Heathen' . . . 'Savage' . . . and finally applied to other peoples."[9]

In the process of classification, these words were first used as an adjective and later became a substantive. Whether or not these words honestly correspond to the reality, they are used and evaluated in reference to Western cultural values. Smith also reminds us that "each of these terms has been applied both to 'others' without and to those perceived as 'others' within."[10] The other remains relative to self, because the boundary between center and periphery is ubiquitous. It exists everywhere, and consequently, it defines the space of human activities.

The last one is concerned with how the other is represented in linguistic terms. Traditionally, language is a marker that identifies who is a member of the community and who is not. This happens also in the biblical world. Smith observes that "within the Hebrew Bible . . . linguistic diversity along with genealogy and territory are the central criteria for ethnic classification

7. Smith, *Relating Religion*, 232.

8. Smith, *Relating Religion*, 234.

9. Smith, *Relating Religion*, 236–37.

10. Smith, *Relating Religion*, 237.

(Gen 10:32, cf. 10:5, 20, 31)."[11] Most often, language is associated with an all-encompassing system of domination.[12] What is troubling is that language has become a determining factor for one's "intelligibility."[13] Smith postulates that anyone who speak a foreign language is deemed "unintelligible and will remain so."[14] Take the Greeks as an example. Smith explains, "Their most fundamental anthropological dualism was linguistic: the *Hellene* who spoke rational speech in opposition to the onomatopoeic *barbarian* . . . who spoke unintelligible, stammering, animal- or child-like speech."[15] The assertion that some languages are objectively better than the others is totally absurd and it presents nothing but a form of hierarchy in opposition to other linguistic systems. It is easy to say inflammatory words, but it is not easy to confront ignorance and arrogance embedded in those words. Smith says poignantly,

> Difference becomes insignificant, in the strict sense of the term and, therefore, requires no decipherment, no exegetical labor, no hermeneutic projects. It is for the vocal opposite, for "us," to speak for "them." Difference has become in-difference. . . . The "other" is represented as mute and unable to speak or, at best, can only, like a parrot, mindlessly mimic their vocal opposite.[16]

While criticizing the imposition of a rigid identity on the other, Smith is convinced that difference is "an ontological cleavage rather than an anthological distinction."[17] The language of the other is a taboo. Its otherness potentially hinders meaningful interactions and communication between self and other, center and periphery, and those who name and the named. Difference is therefore not a cause to celebrate, but a reason to conquer. The difference of the other including the body and mind is subjected to a variety of ideological maneuvers which only sabotages the subjectivity of an individual.

Cultural Difference: A Constructed Discourse

Is difference a bad thing? You and I can be different persons. We have different personalities, characters, and preferences and so on. We differ also in

11. Smith, *Relating Religion*, 239.
12. Smith, *Relating Religion*, 239.
13. Smith, *Relating Religion*, 231.
14. Smith, *Relating Religion*, 237.
15. Smith, *Relating Religion*, 238.
16. Smith, *Relating Religion*, 238–39.
17. Smith, *Relating Religion*, 241.

our worldviews and political choices. What's the fuss about being different? Apparently, it is not about difference, but how we perceive and present the notion of difference.

The discourse of difference becomes another story when it comes to ontological speculation. Inappropriate use of difference to describe social relations will negatively affect how one perceives the other and how one treats the other. Difference between individuals is understood in terms of what something is not or what the other is lacking. The term, "cultural difference," can best illustrate the gap between self and other in relation to a process of differentiation for governing purposes. Cultural difference refers to the variation between cultures. In reality, it is a Western-based expression used to indicate how other cultures diverge from the West.

Speaking against prejudicial perceptions, Homi Bhabha points out that difference in particular cultural difference is a "constructed discourse," deliberately used for political ends. Bhabha postulates, "Cultural difference is a particular constructed discourse at a time when something is being challenged about power or authority. At that point, a particular cultural trait or tradition . . . becomes the site of contestation, abuse, insult, and discrimination." culture."[18]

Bhabha is not interested in studying the plurality of cultures and the dissimilarity between cultures. He is more concerned with the conceptualization of cultural difference, and the reception of that. Bhabha believes that the entire concept of cultural difference is not normal. Even the term itself is not neutral, linguistically. The continual use of this expression will likely justify the norm of cultural reproduction. He puts forward, "Cultural difference is not the natural emanation of the fact that there are different cultures in the world. It's a much more problematic and sophisticated reproduction of a ritual, a habit, a trait, a characteristic. That reproduction has to bear a whole set of significations, tensions and anxieties."[19]

When cultural difference is placed within the framework of redistribution of goods, the primary purpose of cultural reproduction works to confirm the dominant ideological elements.[20] The concept of the other tends to decimate the other's culture, including their language, customs, beliefs and worldviews. And if culture is everything to a person, the lack in one's culture is equal to the deficiency of the other's personhood.

18. Homi Bhabha, "Staging the Politics of Difference: Homi Bhabha's Critical Literacy," in Olson and Worsham, *Race, Rhetoric, and the Postcolonial*, 16.

19. Bhabha, "Staging the Politics of Difference," 16.

20. Bhabha, "Staging the Politics of Difference," 16.

A Reversal of Conventional Discourse on the Other

Conventional research on the Christian missionary movement tends to highlight the wretchedness and despair of the indigenous. Missionary work has focused on the need of the people, which includes providing material support, monetary gifts and even spiritual nourishment. Overemphasizing the people's scarcity will easily render the people incompetent, useless, unproductive and purposeless. These people are just waiting for rescue and empowerment. In contrast to the deficit-based model, I argue that the indigenous, including but not limited to formerly colonized, potential evangelism targets, and local Christians, are all gifted individuals. They are stronger than we could imagine. In highlighting "the priority of the other," Mark Freeman asserts that we can no longer consider ourselves the source of inspiration. It is not us but they who challenge and broaden our worldviews. So Freeman says, these layers of "existential 'nourishment' have little to do with our selves. They derive instead from what is *other* than self, outside of it."[21] Otherness is an asset that needs to be acknowledged. It is also imperative to see it this way so that we can change the entire discursive system of perceiving the other and otherness. To do that, we need to first address various dilemmas of the narratives that have arisen from the biblical accounts on difference and language.

Contestation: Unveiling the Ideology of Homogeneity

The juxtaposition between the Tower of Babel and the Pentecost now comes into play in the notion of difference. In Genesis 11:1, it says, "Now the whole world had one language and a common speech." The history of humanity is marked by the special features of oneness and commonality. Traditional understanding of the story puts an emphasis on the humanity's rebellious nature. Since the idea of building a city did not come from God, human decision and action were to be blamed for it. The theme of human disobedience justifies God's punishment by mixing up people's languages all over the earth. However, such a reading not only gives an impression that God is wrathful and revengeful, but also discredits the necessity of languages.

As we take a look at verse 3, it goes, "They said to each other, 'Come, let's make brick and bake them thoroughly.'" The use of "let" clearly states that the agenda is a command and not a plea. It underscores the desire of becoming great. Through pushing forward the agenda of building the tallest tower in their place, the people of the same mind want to make themselves

---

21. Freeman, *Priority of the Other*, 4–5.

the subject, of space and time, and of history. Alienation resulting from that kind of anthropocentrism carries a huge cost to social relations. The text does not refer to the diversity of languages as a curse. It is, however, the intent to dominate that matters. Daniela C. Augustine argues that God intervenes by deconstructing "every imperial consciousness."[22] Augustine believes, God's act in confusing people's language is not necessarily devaluing the significance of languages but is opposing "a world order that has eliminated the possibility of other."[23]

The core of problematizing difference or otherness aims to homogenize all cultures and languages in the multicultural and multilingual world. What is also true is that the discourse of difference is made and constantly remade. When difference is constructed to vilify other cultures and languages, the discourse underlies imperialist intentions to subjugate and control. However, nothing in the text says that difference is inherently negative. Difference, instead, is a symbol of resistance to the homogenizing power. Genesis 11:7 describes, "Come, let us go down and confuse their language so they will not understand each other." God's use of "let us" is a counter force to human arrogance. It is a demand out of an urge to dismantle habitual subjugation taking place in human society. In the meantime, the act of God manifests a way of life that takes precedence over the life of the other. Augustine also asserts that God in God's plurality of personhood "creates the possibility of an authentic human community, one in which life can be shared together in a multiplicity of forms and locations."[24] The act of God forces one to move away from focusing on self, but recognizes the well-being of the other in the *oikos* of God. The agenda in the household of God always prioritizes the other. Making space for the other highlights the message of love. This language of love expressed in the form of justice and mercy overpowers the language of domination.

To overturn negative perceptions of difference and diversity, one cannot isolate the story of the Tower of Babel but must juxtapose that with the text of the Pentecost in Acts 2. As mentioned, God's intervention against human arrogance represents God's justice and mercy for the world. Justice and mercy embodied in the love of God is pouring out to many but not just a few. This vision of inclusivity that leads to a re-ordering of relationships is affirmed at the Pentecost. Acts 2:1 says, "When the day of Pentecost came, they were all together in one place." When the people gather together,

22. Daniela C. Augustine, "Pentecost as the Church's Cosmopolitan Vision of Global Civil Society," in Storrar, Casarella, and Metzger, *World for All?*, 201.

23. Augustine, "Pentecost as the Church's Cosmopolitan Vision," 202.

24. Augustine, "Pentecost as the Church's Cosmopolitan Vision," 201.

they do not speak about the language of power. As they are gathered by the power of the Holy Spirit, the people are able to speak their own languages. They are not ashamed of who they are, which is a crucial step to establish people's agency and subjectivity. Speaking a foreign language is particularly significant in the Hellenistic world in which Greek is considered the most intelligible form of language. The event at Pentecost invalidates the discourse of Babel on "oneness." That is why Augustine concludes that "Pentecost authenticates the redemption accomplished by God on behalf of humanity in Christ Jesus . . . through the agency of the Holy Spirit."[25] Thus the day of Pentecost is also a day to declare God's mighty deeds of recognizing personhood among individuals. Pentecost gives new prospects for the joy of being different, as it continues to celebrate the vitality, richness and intelligibility of people across cultures and languages. Speaking in one's own tongue and precisely, the diversity of voices concretizes what it means to "Let everything that breathes praise the LORD."

Subversion: Otherness as Gift

Same attracts same. This ends up drawing a boundary between insider and outsider. However, difference helps us think out of the box, and to envision what God has done in every person and every location. The manifold witnesses to God's faithfulness can only be achieved by difference. As it stands, otherness has subverted the discourse on the promise of God. Full inclusion of the other in the household of God becomes necessary. Otherness should not lead to shame and guilt. Otherness is to be respected. It is not only the basis for an authentic human community, but also materializes God's love for the whole world. Otherness, as a symbol of resistance, speaks against the ideology of homogeneity that attempts to objectify and impose constricting rules on other human beings.

Otherness is subversive. The subversive nature of otherness gives a whole new meaning to Christian mission. Building on the Pentecostal event, every single one is a gifted individual. Every single one is empowered with the ability to speak, pray, and sing. Speaking a foreign language does not make one less intelligible. But the multiple voices become a cause to celebrate, for all people are gathered to praise for the greatness of God. Psalm 150:6 says, "Let everything that breathes praise the LORD." All human beings, irrespective of difference, are encouraged and allowed to express their gratitude to the Lord in their own languages. Any responsible missiological approach to a community of people cannot lose sight of the value of the

25. Augustine, "Pentecost as the Church's Cosmopolitan Vision," 204.

people. To pose this idea even more strongly, 'otherness as gift' ought to be an emergent perspective for the task of missiological re-imagination.

Before exploring the topic of otherness as gift, I want to address some confusion about the idea of "gift." Marion Grau postulates that

> the gift can appear as a *pharmakon*, both "the remedy and the poison" for a disease. The gift can enrich and impoverish, poison and heal, the communities it moves between. While "traditional gift exchange is an agent of social cohesion," there are gifts that challenge the "demands of the collective" in such a way that roles become shifted, technologies are introduced, and silences become articulated, while exclusions are challenged. Thus, in many cultures, the gift, like the trickster, can have the function of producing a society or culture to come to terms with new circumstances. It often introduces technologies and cultural innovations crucial for survival, but with a dangerous side. Gift and *pharmakon* "can never be simply beneficial."[26]

Grau's concern is legitimate, as she examines the impact of missionary activities on local cultures. The gift in the form of technological knowhow and material support can adversely affect the character of respective communities and their future development. It also runs the risk of developing the so-called dependency syndrome among the locals. In a sense, the gift is not really free. It comes with certain conditions. Chances are the integrity of local culture will be traded or betrayed in exchange for certain benefits. Because of the ambivalence of a gift, Grau argues that "a "true" gift must be without strings attached, and hence also from an im/possible . . . absolute gift."[27]

Unlike Grau, my argument is that otherness as gift does not consider gift as a thing. The gift of otherness is not something to be consumed and commoditized. It is not even loaded with essentialist connotations. We cannot define the other in terms of essence, or we render the other a means to enlighten the self. It will further intensify self-other binary by subjecting the other to the authority of self. The irreducibility of the other, as Levinas put forward, makes the other incomprehensible. The discourse on otherness is not a matter of categorization: If it does not mean this, it must be that. Seeing otherness as gift is not an alternative. It is inevitable in our relationships with the other.

To reverse prevailing discourses on the other that focus on the deficit of the other, we need to acknowledge the value of the other unconditionally.

---

26. Grau, *Rethinking Mission in the Postcolony*, 213.

27. Grau, *Rethinking Mission in the Postcolony*, 216.

We cannot pass judgment on others, simply based on our moral standards. Just as Grau says, a true gift comes "without strings attached." The discourse that otherness as gift is an unconditional recognition of the other. The other does not need to prove to be something else, in order to receive their deserved dignity. This statement forces us to acknowledge the intrinsic value of the other. I will explain that in detail later in the section. But in the meantime, we all have to agree that implicit bias against otherness is hard to be detected in the dominant structure. The discourse that sees otherness as gift speaks against the representative of the lack through linguistic negation.

While centering on the life of others, the new direction lifts up the intrinsic value of individuals. This project aims to destabilize the efforts of evoking fear and anxiety against the other. When we change the discursive system, we mean to bring in a new set of social behaviors that can build mutuality between one another. Coming back to what Homi Bhabha says earlier, the language of difference pertains to the production of meaning. Interpretation matters. It is a space to contest and subvert preconceived knowledge. Bhabha calls that the Third Space. Bhabha writes,

> The intervention of the Third Space, which makes the structure of meaning and reference an ambivalent process, destroys this mirror of representation in which cultural knowledge is continuously revealed as an integrated, open, expanding code. Such an intervention quite properly challenges our sense of the historical identity of cultural as a homogenizing, unifying force, authenticated by the originary Past, kept alive in the national tradition of the People. In other words, the disruptive temporality of enunciation displaces the narrative of the Western nation.[28]

In challenging the "given" knowledge, Third Space opens to a re-interpretation of the given knowledge. Bhabha says that "even the same signs can be appropriated, translated, rehistoricized, and read anew."[29] Most importantly, this space bridges the gap between one another. Bhabha asserts, "It is in this space that we will find those words with which we can speak of Ourselves and Others."[30] With a similar motivation, Gayati Chakravorty Spivak argues that the change in perspective might be able to dismantle "elite historiography," but it is more significant to affirm "that the agency of change is

---

28. Homi K. Bhabha, "Cultural Diversity and Cultural Differences," in Ashcroft, Griffiths, and Tiffin, *The Post-Colonial Studies Reader*, 156.

29. Bhabha, "Cultural Diversity and Cultural Differences," 157.

30. Bhabha, "Cultural Diversity and Cultural Differences," 157.

located in the insurgent or the "subaltern."[31] Building on these insights, the discourse that sees otherness as gift provides the space to rethink, re-affirm, and re-imagine the identities of the other in Christian missionary activities.

The Poor Evangelizes the Rich

The concept of otherness as gift is not abstract at all. Let us consider the following examples, concerning the relationships between Christians and their neighbors. First, in Russell Jeung's work titled *At Home in Exile: Finding Jesus among My Ancestors and Refugee Neighbors*, Jeung readily shares his experience of living among "the poor." Driven by his evangelical zeal, Jeung moved to the extremely poor zip code in California. A substantial number of Cambodian families have lived in the neighborhood. "Twenty years after the Khmer Rouge's genocidal purge of its people, my neighbors still experienced the trauma of the Killing Fields," says Jeung. Contrary to disparaging these people, Jeung shows the possibility of how otherness puts to shame egotistic missionary strategies. Reclaiming his Hakka cultural roots enables Jeung to see his own vulnerability amid the hospitality of the other.[32] Jeung asserts, "Despite these impoverished conditions and the financial struggles of the Oak Park families, our communal life was rich with social capital: bonds of trust and reciprocity," and "spiritual capital: life that was intimate with God and values that sustained us through struggle."[33]

As Jeung continues his faith journey, he opens himself to the wisdom of the other. A woman from the neighborhood says, "We were all poor; we knew we were poor. But we had fun. We had . . . life!"[34] Jeung does not romanticize poverty. He intentionally recorded and wrote down the people's stories, feelings, and experiences. While attending to the voice of these gracious people, Jeung effectively unveils the entrenched poverty in the United States and its false promise of capitalism. Equally important, Jeung tries to see the world through the eyes of the other. Through living in the reality with the people he values, they envision together a larger reality that is life-giving and life-sustaining.

The transformation that Jeung goes through is not about his being able to know and comprehend the challenges of these poor people, but his being

---

31. Landry and MacLean, *Spivak Reader*, 205–8.

32. Jeung, *At Home in Exile*, 50–51.

33. Jeung, *At Home in Exile*, 35.

34. Jeung, *At Home in Exile*, 35.

able to experience hope in the midst of the people. So Jeung summarizes, "This poor but fun, rich life showered the blessings of the kingdom on me."[35]

The Intelligibility of the Other: Religious Language and Practice

Another case we found in Paul Rajashekar's personal reflection on the relationships with his Hindu neighbors. With sincerity and honesty, Rajashekar recalls,

> I was often appalled to see Hindu gods and goddesses portrayed in the form of idols with multiple hands, eyes, and heads in temples and in pictorial representations. Not only do they look grotesque, but it also seemed absurd to me to worship and venerate deities made out of stone or metal. I often thought of Hindus as idol worshippers, until I met a Hindu scholar who taught me that God is "formless" and genderless but we humans require "forms," "images," and "symbols" as instruments to imagine and conceptualize God. It is not that Hindus worship idols, for they know that idols are human creations, but idols point to a reality that is beyond human grasp. Hindu gods and goddesses are therefore portrayed with multiple hands, heads, and eyes in order to remind of the omnipotence, omnipresence, and omniscience of God. . . . Little did I know the depth of Hindu reflections of God and their approaches to God. I was wrong in assuming or imposing Jewish/Christian/Islamic prejudice toward any forms of idolatry upon Hindus.[36]

The difference between a Christian and a Hindu does not make the individual an obstacle to overcome. But because of the difference, one wishes to get to know the other. Receiving the other may seem to be an activity, but this activity does not exist in and of itself. The act of receiving has to be experienced. It cannot be reduced to receiving some facts about the other, so one can unearth new knowledge about the other. But it is about showing a genuine interest in the life of the other, and receiving another individual with an intention to build friendship, trust and intimacy with the other. The act of receiving is also inviting the other in our midst, so "we" can journey together in search of greater truth.

Rajashekar insists that we are "indebted" to the other. While speaking against the privatization of faith, Rajashekar makes clear that our religious

---

35. Jeung, *At Home in Exile*, 35.

36. J. Paul Rajashekar, "Our God and Their God," in LaHurd, Jadock, and Lohre, *Engaging Others, Knowing Ourselves*, 135.

expression and theological discourse are dependent on the religiosity of the other. Fear of the Lord is universal for human beings across cultures, languages, and religions. The way one worships and praises God can become an anchor point for other religious traditions. Christian pietism does not emerge from a vacuum. Christians receive and appropriate insights from other religions. Thus Rajashekar contends,

> Christians do not have a monopoly on the holy. We recognize this in our indebtedness to Judaism. We, in fact, have borrowed prayers from that tradition. In our communal worship we frequently use the Jewish psalter, and together with Jews we sing praises to the Lord. . . . Christians have been doggedly loyal to the Hebrew Scriptures. . . . The Hebrew psalmody is undeniably a source of spiritual enrichment for Christians of all ages. Together with Jews we have unreservedly affirmed the call to pray found in Psalm 150:6: "Let everything that breathes praise the Lord" (NRSV). . . . In doing so we acknowledge that like breath, prayer is a human need, an expression of our finitude, a search for relationship with the One who is beyond us all. Because we human beings are creatures who are mere mortals, must suffer, are ignorant, and in pain, everywhere human beings have reached out to a transcendent Other that might help them out of their mortality, redeem them from their suffering, enlighten their ignorance, heal their pain, grant them forgiveness, or liberate them from their bondage. . . . Prayer is a common act to reach out beyond ourselves.[37]

So the religiosity of the other puts to shame our assumptions about people, particularly whose faith is different from our own tradition. Their experience and practice challenge our faith by relativizing the absoluteness in our knowledge of God and the world. The religiousness of the other tells us that we do not have an advantage to epistemology. Their voices has concretized the concept of humanization that further enriches the meaning of salvation in Christianity. The Christian conviction that God's grace is universal becomes more substantial. Furthermore, the claim that "prayer is a common act to reach out beyond ourselves" sends us out to the world and inspires us to deepen our conversation about ethical obligations with one another.

---

37. Rajashekar, "Our God and Their God," 129.

Full Personhood of the Other

Affirming otherness as gift cannot be reduced to receiving an individual who can increase my intellectual capacity. Otherwise, relationship becomes functional. The affirmation is not an affirmation at all. Affirming otherness as gift means, acknowledging full personhood of other individuals. It is problematic to say, one can accept the plurality of religions without respecting the way people think, act, and talk. People's identities and subjectivities are entangled with their land, their social systems, and their religion. Sociologist Meredith McGuire uses the term "lived religion" to refer to "how religion and spirituality are practiced, experienced, and expressed by ordinary people (rather than official spokespersons) in the context of their everyday lives."[38] McGuire goes on to explain, "Instead of understanding religion as a separate component of human life and action that remains distinct from other aspects of everyday life, lived religion defines the religions as that engagement with sacred dimensions of life which finds expression in the everyday experience of people."[39]

We simply cannot focus on either the religious aspect of an individual or the experiences and feelings of the individual. None of them are separable bodily from the other. As their religion operates within the framework of their worldview, their faith is neatly incorporated into the person's entirety of life. Gavin Flood puts an emphasis on the mediation of language. He asserts that "the story of a person's life, what gives us meaning and purposes, what determines our meaningful relationships with each other, is formed through . . . language." Language that embodies both "the person and subjectivity" enables and guides "the body" to worship God. So when we affirm otherness as gift, we respect this "lived religion" closely observed by members of the wider community. We also acknowledge their use of religious language and practice, and their subjectivities.

What they value in life and how they do things are inextricably linked, and the expression of who they are is precisely an exercise of their human agency. As illustrated in Rajashekar's encounter with the Hindu, the Hindu scholar talked back and resisted the onslaught of the Christian-centric worldview by demonstrating the wisdom of his religion. The Hindu scholar did not surrender his religion to the scrutiny of the other. Their self-worth and self-confidence surpassed those expectations and norms that have been imposed on them. The other does not have to be a Christian to be "human" and to practice humanity. The presence of the other further reflects

38. McGuire, *Lived Religion*, 12.
39. McGuire, *Lived Religion*, 12.

the beauty of *imago dei,* which is to declare that the other is made in the image of God.

Acknowledging the agency and subjectivity of the other makes a powerful announcement that the other is an active participant in human history. That can effectively question existing power structures that are favorable to the Anglo-European linguistic systems. The resistance against submitting oneself to dominant structures also prevents one's identity from being compromised in the civilizing mission.

Recognizing the other's full personhood will furthermore lead us to the path toward intersubjectivity. The center of Christianity is not one. It is many. We are not defined by a single cultural-linguistic system that domesticates the revelation of God. All people, regardless of languages, cultures, and religions, sing praises to God, for the grace of God bestows on us through varied mysterious ways. The discourse that Western Christianity, including Western cultural values and epistemological categories, is the center has collapsed. There is nothing to celebrate but there is much to ponder in the present and the future. We need to build relationships. But we also need to build closeness. The sense of connection cultivated through intersubjective relationships is urgently needed.

Space is not defined by what Christians are doing. But what Christians and others are doing in space, including their activities and communication are all materialized in the sociality. Intersubjective relationships are dynamic in nature. People are not related as thinking beings. They are rather interrelated as social beings or subjects of experience. Mutual transformation takes place when people truly respect the lived experience of one another. The interaction that aspires to people's agency and subjectivity shall transcend boundaries that are objectively created to segregate. Seeing otherness as gift can essentially re-map the reality of space and turn it into a space for possibility.

Summary

"Who is the other?" "Who are the people we 'serve' in the so-called mission field?" "What does otherness mean to us?" All these questions do not aim to elicit information, so that we can make statement about the other. Instead, they intend to stimulate our thinking and forge intimacy between one another, or help us connect to other human beings we meet face-to-face on a daily basis.

Ontological differences among people of different cultures and communities are not going to disappear. Biblical accounts on difference and language have subverted conventional discourse on otherness. The presence of the other informs us that the thinking and approaches we have cherished for ages are already obsolete. People who are deemed the other are by no means inferior to us. They are human beings. They are gifted individuals. They are irreducible. Otherness should not be a threat to overcome. Otherness is subversive.

The discourse of otherness as gift therefore represents a significant departure that breaks away from abstract concepts and distancing theological orientation. Our missiological discourse should stand firm in shattering binary opposites and building healthy relationships. The radical shift in the discourse on other and otherness will bring together all people created by God, and together we can journey by faith in search of greater truth.

6

The Promise of Emergent Language

Re-imagining the Way Forward

> Words, when they are living and breathing, are like musical chords. . . . Words and sentences, like people, are forever in motion . . . it means to bring a person, a feeling, an idea, to life.[1]

THIS CHAPTER CONSISTS OF two major sections. In the first part, I will introduce a new language that runs counter to negative stereotypes. The new language will create an inclusive narrative for missionary work, by facilitating mutuality and allowing ongoing dialogue with our neighbors. While these features and dimensions are required for a new narrative to be credible, I emphasize that our missiological language needed to take root in God's reconciling love. Reconciliation defines what God has done and is doing in the world, and God's reconciliation should help us envision a responsible discourse that rightly speaks power and justly considers the difference between individuals. In the final section, I will give my concluding remarks concerning the connection between language and the future of Christian mission. Today's world is dominated by bigoted discourses, lies, and half-truths against all forms of life. We recognize that linguistic implications preserve supremacist attitudes. We need to challenge ourselves to cross the boundary set for the other. We need to stop creating any narrative that benefits a few and targets the majority other. Our language for Christian mission in the

---

1. Thomas Ogden believes one of the biggest challenges to contemporary psychoanalysis is to express the intricacies of human experience through language. The experience between analyst and analysand should never be static. The analysand does not necessarily play a passive role during interview. Language is able to create a situation in which people can listen to themselves. What they say and what they hear are inseparable of how they feel. When the people listen to what they say, they can express their true feelings. Language is crucial to bringing life to the entire analytic process. Ogden, *Reverie and Interpretation*, 4–5.

twenty-first century will truly affirm the value of the other and reestablish broken relationships between one another.

A New Language for Christian Mission: Re-imagining the Way Forward

Missiological language cannot be rested upon abstract and theoretical theology, but arises out of genuine and sincere interactions with the other in their cultures and languages. If language, as John Searle says, has the capacity to create a reality, language should be able to create a space to embrace. It can help us cross the boundaries that shut people out. Rethinking our language is necessary for the task of missiological re-imagination.

First of all, what do I mean by a new language? Does it mean a brand new language that has never existed in human history? When it comes to "new," I do not mean something that has never ever happened before. Edward Said reminded us that certain forms of value judgment are already embedded in the thing that is designated as new as opposed to "not-new" and the new/not-new dichotomy is arbitrary.[2] The premise that the new should replace the old is just another case of imposition of values. "New" can turn out to be a form of linguistic propaganda that espouses self-aggrandizing projects.

To effectively tackle the deep-seated problem of the invisible other, a new language epitomizes much-needed new thinking. Living in new horizons thus entails an abandonment of biased assumptions about the other—including but not limited to the way the other goes about doing things. It opens our eyes to see our own weakness, and through that enlightenment, it welcomes other possibilities of understanding the reality. New thinking thus means conceptualizing anew our way of engaging in our church and larger communities, while trying to be faithful to the vision of God disclosed in the life of the other. A new language represents the commitment to break down the walls of division. It means building trust, fostering relationship, and sustaining constructive mutual interaction.

---

2. Edward Said might refer to the function of textuality when examining the units of knowledge. But he believed knowledge is not accumulated through the text alone. He says, "Criticism cannot assume that its province is merely the text. . . . It must see itself, with other discourse, inhabiting a much contested cultural space, in which what has counted in the continuity and transmission of knowledge has been the signifier, as an event that has left lasting traces upon the human subject" (*World, the Text, and the Critic,* 180–81).

Speaking the Language of Reconciliation

I have said this many times, that language can do harm, but language can also heal. Using language is a learned social behavior. It is necessary to shun offensive language. But ensuring that our language—both written and spoken—is appropriate and non-discriminatory is not enough. Language used for Christian witness and the life of discipleship should first take heed to the aspect of reconciliation.

The rhetoric of reconciliation, nowadays, is often associated with restoring peace and order in respective communities after civil war and ethnic strife. I do not dispute that since violence-related injuries and deaths constantly grab the headlines. This gives currency to anything that Christians say about the ministry of reconciliation. Thus conventional discourse on reconciliation tends to accentuate the role of mission agencies and societies as peace-maker. That image of the church as the "reconcilers" who "bring hope for all" was imprinted in the WCC Vancouver Assembly 1983, and it becomes remarkably popular even to this day.[3]

There are, however, more facets in the discussion of healing communities. This holds true in particular in circumstances where gospel-bearers exclude and subjugate non-Christians in the name of Christianity. Missionary activities are often guilty of setting up the indigenous as the other of Christians, and evaluate them only relative to Christians. In short, they are secondary and inferior to Christians. There are other occasions when missioner—covertly and overtly—fragmented justice in the interests of civilizing mission. In a sense, mission societies and agencies do not have the privilege to oversee how justice is being served. A better way for them to get involved in the ministry of reconciliation is to repair broken relationships and reestablish relationships with the other.

Since people are confused about their role in reconciliation, it is timely and relevant to remind ourselves with the message of reconciliation. It is written in 2 Corinthians 5:19 that "in Christ God was reconciling the world to himself, not counting their trespasses against them, and entrusting the message of reconciliation to us." The text specifies that reconciliation takes root in God and is originated from God. So Colin E. Gunton insists, God is "the author of reconciliation."[4] It is God who takes the initiative to reconcile the world to Godself. Reconciliation is, first and foremost, an act of God concerning the relations between God and the world. Reconciliation thus contains the important message about God's love and faithfulness by

3. WCC, "Statement on the Middle East (10 August 1983)."

4. Gunton, *Theology of Reconciliation*, 2.

reestablishing broken relationships with humanity and the world. God does not need the world to reconcile the world to Godself; rather, God reconciled the world to Godself for the sake of us and the world. Gunton says it well, God is "being the *mediatorial* rather than *penal* substitution whereby God himself (sic) re-establishes the communion which was broken by human sin."[5]

This message of reconciliation was first a divine action, and now becomes a reality that obliges and motivates us to do to our neighbors. The gospel of Jesus Christ that reconciles people to God reconciles also people to people. Svetlana Khobnya puts it, "Reconciliation is . . . theologically/Christologically as God's act in Christ and missiologically as the ministry of reconciliation of those who are in Christ."[6] Christian mission or missiological exploration is theologically and biblically grounded in God's reconciling act to the world. The ministry of reconciliation becomes the identity of Christ's followers.

In line with Khobnya's argument that reconciliation "has both personal/communal ('reconciled us' v. 18) and universal ('the world' v. 19) dimensions," I consider two levels of reconciliation that need our attention. They are the inner and outer levels. Both of them are interconnected. The former focuses on motivations and attitudes; while, the latter has practical implications for healthy interpersonal relationships. True reconciliation entails an act of repentance. To repent is more than apologizing for our wrongdoing. Repentance requires us to turn to God. It is not simply about doing, but also being. Turning ourselves 180 degrees means we believe not in our power and strength, but in the faithfulness of God promised for all.

Martin Marty rightly connects repentance with "a change of heart," in commemorating the five hundredth anniversary of the Protestant Reformation.[7] Marty highlights the first thesis that Martin Luther wrote: "When our Lord and Master Jesus Christ said, 'Repent' (Matthew 4:17), he intended the entire life of believers to be repentance."[8] Repentance does not focus on a specific area of life, but the entirety of life. There is no intellectual repentance; for a change of heart is a total change of an individual. He or she holds nothing back. Even that change is bestowed through a form of grace; no one can do anything of it or boast of anything, but repent. Furthermore, repentance is not required specifically of non-Christians, but of all believers of God. This applies, in particular, to those who are preaching the message of

---

5. Gunton, *Theology of Reconciliation*, 2.

6. Khobnya, "Reconciliation Must Prevail," 129

7. Marty, *October 31, 1517*, 5.

8. Marty, *October 31, 1517*, 4–5.

repentance to the so-called religious other. Focusing too much on the other's weakness does not make us more righteous; instead, our self-righteousness through thoughts, words and deeds has already caused harm to others.

It may be a little too general to say—though it is true—that heart matters, and it matters most to God. The absence of that in the work of reconciliation will suggest that one tries to repent without really repenting. In his award-winning book *Exclusion & Embrace*, Miroslav Volf deepens the meaning of reconciliation. Although Volf prioritizes forgiveness in reconciliation, he does not lose sight of the purity of heart. Volf underlines Jesus' reactions against the hypocrisy of religious leaders on the observance of rituals and laws. By challenging the practice of exclusion, Volf asserts that self-identity is often overlapped with power. Thus Volf concludes that "evil does not lie outside of a person, in impure things, but inside a person, in the impure heart (Mark 7:15) . . . the *pursuit of false purity* emerges as a central aspect of sin. . . . Sin is here the kind of purity that wants the world cleansed of the other rather than the heart cleansed of the evil.[9]

Repentance and the cleansing of one's heart become an important part of Volf's theology of embrace. In a similar vein, Desmond Tutu says, "True reconciliation is based on forgiveness, and forgiveness is based on true confession."[10] Given the challenging past in South Africa, Archbishop Tutu never minces his words. Admitting one's error, brutality, and transgression is never easy, and yet Tutu insists that forgiveness is difficult without that step. Tutu also mentions repentance and forgiveness will inevitably be followed by reparation. He uses the example of Apartheid to illustrate how the life of the transgressed is solidly and negatively impacted arising from conflicts. Tutu says, "Apartheid provided the whites with enormous benefits and privileges, leaving its victims deprived and exploited."[11] Something needs to be done to address the livelihood of the people and to restore relationships between the conflicting parties. Thus Tutu claims, "We must go to the root, remove that which is festering, cleanse and cauterize, and then a new beginning is a possibility."[12]

True reconciliation leads to a change in motivations and attitudes, which implies that we dare to live ourselves into new ways of thinking and the new thinking will help renew our ethical ways of relating to the other. Acts of reconciliation will start from our use of language. I have shown that language not only conveys ideas but also constructs a reality. Language

9. Volf, *Exclusion & Embrace*, 74.

10. Tutu, *God Has a Dream*, 53.

11. Tutu, *God Has a Dream*, 57.

12. Tutu, *God Has a Dream*, 53–54.

becomes a mediating space for self and other. It is the interactions between these two parties that constitute the self and form corresponding ethical obligation for the other. One fundamental step is to discard the narrative that belittles the other and pursue a new one that sustains communal wellbeing for the present and future.

The eighth commandment that says "You shall not bear false witness against your neighbor" (Exodus 20:16; Deuteronomy 5:20, NRSV) offers the best insights for us to develop an appropriate communicative process with the other in pluralistic contexts. The resurgence of other world religions poses a threat to the Christian community. A common reaction to someone whose religion is strange to us is to deny the validity of his or her religious tradition and thus the value of that person. Driven by ignorance and misunderstandings, Christians easily apply judgments, such as "They are devil," "They believe in false teachings," "Their religion is built on lies," and the list goes on. By vilifying people of other faiths to be demon or unauthentic, the negative image intends to spread hatred among Christians and persuade them to join the cause of soul saving. Some of these insults are unfortunately meant to seek political influence.[13]

In exploring peace-making practices, Craig Nessan asserts that "the church is called to the *practice of interpreting the actions of others in the kindest way.*"[14] The task of interpreting the actions of others requires us to recognize the humanity and dignity of other individuals."[15] They are human beings like us. No one should be treated differently. It is never right to disparage people based on their religious conviction. Reconciliation is not only about equality, but also about breaking the pattern of transgression and destructive behaviors. As Nessan argues, "The seeds of human violence are often sown through the use of language to demean and degrade others."[16] Basically, we have to be cautious about the way we talk about others and communicate with them. But that is not enough. To build on Martin Luther's idea, Nessan adds, we need to stand by the other and "speak well of them" whenever possible.[17] Nessan also reminds us, "The body of Christ is summoned to speak charitably about others, interpreting their actions in the best possible way. The choice to do so counteracts spirals of violence, not only in the church but in society."[18]

---

13. Tutu, *God Has a Dream*, 53–54.

14. Nessan, "Cross as Foundation," 103.

15. Nessan, "Cross as Foundation," 103.

16. Nessan, "Cross as Foundation," 103.

17. Nessan, "Cross as Foundation," 103.

18. Nessan, "Cross as Foundation," 103.

We use our tongues to bring blessings to others. Mutual transformation will happen when people learn to embrace the other and otherness. Rabbi Arthur Waskow goes a step further to suggest that one can see the face of God through the face of others.[19] In his writing titled *The Torah of Esau and Jacob, Gaza and Israel*, Rabbi Waskow deepens the concept of "the face of God" by drawing reference to the wrestling between Jacob and the divine being. In wrestling with the divine being, Jacob saw the face of God. Jacob internalized the experience of encountering the divine face-to-face. When he met Esau the following day, Jacob said to Esau face-to-face that "To see your face is like seeing God's Face." Rabbi Waskow believes, "He (Jacob) is transformed. And then Esau is transformed as well. When he sees that Jacob has been transformed, Esau withholds his power. He chooses peace rather than a 'legitimate' retribution for the wrong that has been done him. The brothers embrace." Rabbi Waskow might have used the story to talk about the issue between Gaza and Israel, but his exegesis on the story sheds new light on the feasibility of mutual transformation in the midst of reconciliation. No one has seen the face of God. But if the face of the other reflects the glory of God, what would we do to and for the other? When the other sees that self has been transformed, would not the other restrain his/her power to fight back, and make possible a renewal of relations?

Reconciliation defines what God is doing in the world, so God's reconciling work lays the foundation for our engagement with the other. The language of Christian mission should build on God's reconciling love to and for the world. Our language will no longer be the language of damnation and domination, but one that embraces difference and diversity. We are called to make peace. Peace-making does not put us on a morally higher ground, but urges us to reestablish broken relationships with the other on a daily basis and face-to-face contexts. Without the step of being reconciling individuals, we do not know the priority of missionary work. When reconciliation truly takes place, there will be a change of hearts. Transformation will instigate further transformations happening within ourselves and the world.

19. Rabbi Arthur Waskow founded the Shalom Center in 1983. His reflection on the Torah of Esau and Jacob was written in the midst of the Gaza-Israel war in 2012. He believed the story could help both governments of Gaza and Israel to make a better choice in addressing issues and hatred between them. See Waskow, "Torah of Esau and Jacob."

Language That Facilitates Mutuality

Two other features of the emergent missiological language are derived from the basis of God's reconciling love. They include mutuality and ongoingness. First, the principle of mutuality necessitates a language of "we." Human beings are relational. When we fail to take note of that, the world will only become a world of *you* and a world of *I*. There is no meaningful interaction between the two. Kenneth J. Gergen says, "If there were no pronouns, would *you* and *I* cease to exist as independent beings? Would there be an *I* if there were no means of designating a separate being? To employ the words *you* and *I* is to create a world of separations."[20]

This is an important message for those who are engaging in Christian missionary work. In a dichotomized world, we are so tempted to divide people into I the Christian and you the non-Christian. Shifting the individualistic language to one that respects the agency and subjectivity of the other becomes central to missiological orientation and construction.

Mutual learning will never take place when one just sits there and makes statements about the other, including the way people look, speak, and do things. Listening to the story of the other is an effective way to expose oneself to the complexity of situations. Felix Ehimare Enegho and Friday John Imekh send a clear message to missionaries who come to their land that language of compulsion only jeopardizes missionary activities.[21] This kind of language is ethnocentric and at times, destructive to indigenous cultures. In Thomas Ogden's words, the language of compulsion represents a form of "lifelessness."[22] Based on his observation of the language used in psychoanalysis, Odgen writes,

> Among the most common that I have encountered is language that derives from dogmatism and ideological loyalties. When ideological bonds are dominant for the analyst, the analyst often adopts (or is adopted by) the language of his analytic "school." Analytic language that is ideological is no longer alive because the answers to the questions being raised are known by the analyst from the outset and the function of language has been reduced to the conveying of that knowledge to the analysand.[23]

20. Gergen, *Relational Being*, 30.

21. Enegho and Imaekhai, "Language and Christian Evangelism," 347.

22. Ogden, *Reverie and Interpretation*, 219.

23. Ogden, *Reverie and Interpretation*, 219.

Ogden contends that all kinds of "stereotypic, cliché-ridden, over-inflated, authoritarian language" are "dead language."[24] Dead language negates people's way of life. While being aware of those dull and immaterial words, the language of decency can help us better understand the challenges people are facing in their contexts and to refrain from moral judgment.

The language of decency does not mean we keep our mouth shut completely; although in some circumstances, we need to do that. I am suggesting that our language should be preceded by the lived experience of the other. As they identify their own discourse through story-telling, their stories change the narrative about them or challenge biased perceptions against them. In the meantime, their stories can change us. Their stories can shape our language and even turn our language upside down, particularly when they strike a chord with the problem in our own culture. We learn to confront past mistakes including self-indulgent and self-serving desires, and also, we learn to be more careful with our offensive language and action, against potential targets of evangelism and even against the less normative group in society. We humble ourselves and learn to be a better person from those we deem as the other.

Mission discourse that pays attention to the stories of others can foster effective intercultural engagement. Intercultural is not understood to be simply an adjective that describes the daily operations of Christian mission, but it is also a form of being that asks the whole body of Christ to share gifts with one another and to reorder priorities in working with others for the healing of the world. Let me back up and explain a little about the prefix "inter-" which is a Latin word, meaning "between," "in the midst of," "mutually," "reciprocally," "together" and so on. When highlighting Christian mission as *inter*-cultural, it indicates that there is a great desire for everyone to make relationships healthier and more functional through mutual respect and learning. In creating constructive cross-cultural interactions, Christena Cleveland suggests that "direct contact between members of different groups will reverse those inaccurate perceptions, negative emotions and discrimination. . . . It also works by forcing individuals to see the similarities between themselves and the other group."[25]

While intercultural engagement concretizes the notion of "otherness as gift," it leads to the realization of intersubjectivity. Concern for the other does not rest on a self-fulfilling monologue, but the voices of others. In *Braided Selves*, Pamela Cooper-White asserts that a genuine collaboration "invites contemplation of the weaving together of multiple parts and

---

24. Ogden, *Reverie and Interpretation*, 224.

25. Cleveland, *Disunity in Christ*, 153–54.

subjectivities in the experience of self and other, and further, implies an on-goingness—braiding is a continual process, and as such supports dynamic and relational views of multiplicity of persons."[26] Clearly as Cooper-White says, relationships complement each other. When both sides abandon their agendas, they abandon also the language used to expand their intellectual capacity only. So "we" will both benefit through a healthy and growing relationship.

Language That Sustains Ongoing Dialogue

Speaking of "ongoingness," it is important for us to understand that relationship is a process and not a result. So the idea that making friends alone will lead one to succeed in the Christian missionary movement is seemingly premature. We are not done yet. Even making friends is not a one-time event. Cultivating friendship takes time and effort. The principles of mutuality and reciprocity also describe a process of growth, alluding to a life-long journey of walking together with the other.

The idea of ongoingness also implies that our dialogue with the other is not limited to those structured ones. Authentic dialogue can happen quietly in the most simple and ordinary moment of life which allows more people to participate and support growth. As mentioned earlier, a lived religion is an integration of people's religious language and practice with their identities and subjectivities. Dialogue happens in people's everyday life: it can be the moment when people are embraced by their circle of friends, or the time when they mourn for the loss of their beloved ones. Dialogue happens in every sacred moment of life.

The Vatican document on dialogue and proclamation offers some helpful insights on "The Forms of Dialogue." The list includes,

a) The dialogue of life, where people strive to live in an open and neighborly spirit, sharing their joys and sorrows, their human problems and preoccupations

b) The dialogue of action, in which Christians and others collaborate for the integral development and liberation of people

c) The dialogue of theological exchange, where specialists seek to deepen their understanding of their respective religious heritages, and to appreciate each other's spiritual values

d) The dialogue of religious experience, where persons, rooted in their own religious tradition, share their spiritual riches, for

26. Cooper-White, *Braided Selves*, 9.

instance with regard to prayer and contemplation, faith and ways of searching for God or the Absolute.[27]

In view of the pluralistic realities in which we are living, the interest in our neighbors, including their religions is not a personal preference. It calls us to break down barriers that keep us apart from the other. In *Not Without My Neighbor*, Wesley Ariarajah makes use of his childhood encounters with his Hindu neighbors to argue that meeting people of other faiths is a daily experience for many Christian communities in Asia.[28] Churches in Asia have to deal with issues about interfaith prayer, interfaith marriage, religion and conflicts every moment every single day. Their minority status in society implies that there is no short cut for churches in Asia to work with their neighbors. Ariarajah critiques that missiological orientation becomes narrow when it concerns only about preaching the gospel and persuading the Hindu neighbors to accept what Christians have believed to be good news. This understanding of mission totally disregards the loving relationship and prayer life that has long been fostered by Christians and Hindus in their daily encounter.

Knowledge is not a closed system. I have mentioned over and over again that Christians do not have "the Truth" to tell. Our conceptualization of the reality is in fact embedded with certain values and assumptions. Our social location, including but not limited to the process of socialization, conditions our understanding of the world and of religion. Our point of view tends to be partial and incomprehensive. When a specific social location becomes the single whole, it easily ignores the particularity and complexity of life. That will subsequently affect the formation of one's behavioral patterns toward the other. Paul Rajashekar suggests how dialogue can happen in power asymmetries. He asserts,

> It is helpful to emphasize that dialogue is essentially an encounter between subjects, not a discussion about objects. The "other tradition," previously an object of polemic and suspicion, has to be seen incarnated in this person, a fellow subject in dialogue. The moment the other becomes a "you," a subject, a human face, and not an anonymous entity, the nature of the problem

---

27. Pontifical Council for Interreligious Dialogue, "Dialogue and Proclamation."

28. Wesley Ariarajah, student of Stanley Samartha, was born in Sri Lanka. He followed in his teacher Samartha's footsteps and became involved in the Interfaith Dialogue Department of the World Council of Churches and later the Deputy General Secretary of the WCC. One of Ariarajah's renowned works, entitled *Not Without My Neighbor: Issues in Interfaith Relations*, highlighted his enthusiasm in bridging the gap between Christians and people of other faiths.

changes. . . . Put differently, it is learning to be guests, not hosts,
in the midst of people of other faiths.[29]

The radical shift of subject/object position in dialogue subverts
power dynamics. Change is inevitable. And this change has two levels of
meaning. First, shifting the hierarchal order between subject and object
provides equality between two parties. They are equal interlocutors. The
sense of equality speaks against the objectification of the other by freeing
the egotistic self from self-seeking purposes; and second, the resulting shift
of relationship empowers and enables the other to assume his or her full
personhood. The subversive nature of dialogue transcends cultural expectations imposed on one another, as both sides seek to discover and expand the
meaning of life togetherness.

To reiterate, the assertion that missionary engagement is dialogical
emphasizes the significance of process and not result. It is not saying that
the result is unimportant. No one can foresee or determine the results of
dialogue. Furthermore, there is no winner or loser when it comes to dialogue. Dialogue with another resembles a quest for greater truth. C. S. Song
reminds us that "our exercise is not to come up with *correct* answers. . . . It is
our hope that as we wrestle with them honestly, we may be led to a deeper
understanding of who we are and to a personal encounter with that loving
power we call God—from whose eternity we came and to whose eternity
we return."[30] When dialogue occurs in the spirit of relationality, it brings
relevance to the life of the other. Ongoing and constructive dialogue encourages mutual transformation that further sustains tolerance, creativity,
and growth among one another.

Concluding Remarks

Language and the Christian missionary movement intersect in complicated
ways to homogenize differences in cross-cultural situations. The world
continues to be dichotomized into the West and the rest. Missiological languages are evaluated within the Western linguistic framework. Prevailing
mission discourses fail to challenge the hierarchical order between cultures
and people.

What is more complex is that injustice takes place at home and abroad.
Hateful speech and the language of bullying have become pervasive in politics. Recently, we have heard enough (and there may be many more to come)

29. Rajashekar, "Faith and the Other," 436.
30. Song, *Tracing the Footsteps of God*, 7.

bigoted, racist, and sexist comments made by the current administration of the United States. The normalization of that is not natural. When inflicting insults on the other finds its way to be part of people's everyday life, the new normal instantly discriminates against people on the basis of difference. In view of the erasure of otherness, Macedo, Dendrinos, and Gounari strongly react to the proposition of "commonness" in the common language and common culture. For them, it is "a euphemism that has been used to describe the imposition of Western dominant culture in order to degrade and devalue any different ethnic/ cultural/ class characteristics."[31] Eliminating difference intends to perpetuate white privilege.[32] In some cases, when a person speaks his or her dialect in public, the person will immediately receive uncomfortable stares or get reprimanded for failing to speak the official language. There are other occasions when Spanish-speakers are ordering food at restaurants in their language, they are scolded and asked to go back to their country. These incidences of linguistic violence happen a lot in the United States. The ideology of commonness, alongside an aggressive assimilationist policy, forcefully severs people's cultural ties and aggravates the identity crisis for immigrants and their children.[33]

Apart from that, suggestions are made in numbers of European countries to require immigrants to stop speaking their native languages even at home. In the United Kingdom, there are debates about whether immigrants who fail to meet the language proficiency requirement should face deportation. Although some say it should only apply to those who want to extend their visas or apply for permanent residence, the excuse for increasing national security in combating domestic extremism targets immigrants, foreigners, and strangers, arbitrarily. The daily discursive practices of reproducing state sanctioned identity only produce more barriers between people and cultures. For that matter, Esme Cleall unhesitatingly connects the notion of difference in the nineteenth-century missionary accounts with current political and religious conditions. From heathen violence to "the location of 'terror' with the other," Cleall believes the West is ferociously re-fortifying its cultural values. The West has advanced its hegemonic state to the level of absolutizing all discourses on good and evil. She blatantly points out that "leader in both the UK and the US have drawn on values of liberty, and also God, to justify their actions."[34] Humiliating words are disseminated for propagandist purposes to intimidate. These same words

---

31. Macedo, Dendrinos, and Gounari, *Hegemony of English*, 37–38.

32. Macedo, Dendrinos, and Gounari, *Hegemony of English*, 37–38.

33. Macedo, Dendrinos, and Gounari, *Hegemony of English*, 37–38.

34. Cleall, *Missionary Discourses of Difference*, 170.

are rippling around the globe. Power differentials between people occur at all levels, everywhere. Many are subject to a deprivation of their freedom and dignity.

What is our response to biased and destructive language that determines events of our era? One thing is certain: Our understanding of Christian mission can rest no longer upon abstract and theoretical theology, but arise out of sincere engagement with the other in their languages and cultures.

Mission is commonly known as sending someone to advance the gospel of Jesus Christ among the unchurched. The notion of sending is largely derived from the mission of God the Father, mission of God the Son, and mission of God the Holy Spirit. This reading strategy easily reinforces the overarching theme of God sending the Son by the power of the Spirit to save the world. While Christian mission is understood within the framework of a single event of salvation, it runs the risk of reducing mission to saving people from wretchedness. This assumption is prevalent in the triumphalist narratives of Western Christian mission. Missionary work targets religious other in the non-Western mission field. Making local converts, developing a local mission, and equipping local partner ministries and the like are emboldening the sense of personal mission. Missionary activities turn out to be a platform for expressing one's individuality.

Christian mission cannot be understood as "sending" alone, particularly when the notion of sending overemphasizes the act of going. There are other important facets of Christian witness, such as "being" and "speaking." Being is a form of witness and speaking is the language we use to proclaim God's love for the world. Both of these dimensions are interrelated. Christian mission, as a form of witness, requires a responsible language to speak about the gospel and the other. In chapter 3, I highlighted Jesus' self-emptying act to counter self-centered motives. Jesus' self-emptying love on the cross confronts violence of any form; his death and resurrection envision a path of transformation. Being centered in God steers us away from being inward-looking and provides the basis for our way of being that further readies us to live a life for the well-being of others. In the newness of life, we reject injustice, including linguistic violence being inflicted on the marginalized communities. Later in chapter 4, I juxtaposed the Tower of Babel with the Pentecostal event to subvert the discourse of difference. The core of problematizing difference or otherness aims to homogenize all cultures and languages in the multicultural and multilingual world. Otherness is not a threat. Otherness, instead, is a symbol of resistance to the homogenizing power. The affirmation that seeing otherness as gift is to restore the people's agency and subjectivities. This emergent discourse can also resist and subvert established narratives that divide and denigrate people of other cultural-linguistic systems.

It has become apparent that other and otherness are important themes for missiological discussion in consideration of power differentials in relationships. Christian missionary work needs to challenge a problematic understanding of self and a biased reading of the other. Christian missionary work has to address relational disorder that exposes deeper issues of epistemological principles, theological orientation and praxis. The approach of contesting and subverting mission discourses does not simply replace one narrative by another. It works to transcend unnecessary stereotypes, thus give justice to the people we work with.

A missionary encounter therefore becomes a space that enables one to meet different and comprehensive visions of life. Encountering other linguistic systems opens a window to explore and appreciate a different culture. Upon missionary encounter, we invite also a wide range of epistemologies that give vivid expressions of the mystery of the Divine. Not only does the encounter challenge us to see God's activities on earth, but also questions the notion that one's own culture is superior to all others. No single linguistic system is complete. Each one contains fundamental metaphors that convey and construct specific kinds of cosmologies and implications for human relationships. The interactions between various linguistic categories of the Absolute will effectively expand creative expressions of God. Christian mission is also an invitation for all people to discover the wondrous work of God.

Anyone who is interested in mission studies or missionary work needs to understand otherness in a positive light. Indeed, most of the local church leaders are working at their home congregations and preaching among their own people. Some of them even reside overseas teaching and ministering at the terrain of their former mission societies and agencies. Current discourses on global mission including their rationale need to be re-evaluated thoroughly. Global mission cannot capitalize on conversion and empowering local Christians to convert the locals. The problems facing our world today are not just about poverty, hunger, pollution, and HIV/AIDS, but also insurgence of Islam, immigration, and terrorism. Easy dichotomization and dehumanization are commonplace to objectify the other. We need to constantly remind ourselves if mission discourses are adequate for creating a reality beyond the construct of self and other. Reflections on self, identity, and mission do not aim at inciting guilt in mission societies and agencies to motivate them to change. The constant process of self-examination, in particular the role of language, is timely and relevant in this very unsettled world.

To renew our commitment to the other, we need to speak against a linguistic framework that forbids the presence of the other, or that reinforces the imposed order and inculcates a sense of inferiority in the people. We need to do more than practice tokenism, or, a symbolic act of giving voice to the underside. We need also to democratize the decision-making process and allow different languages to describe diverse religious experiences and varied conceptions of being human.

Linguistic equality entails a re-ordering of relationships that helps us confront our vainglory and allows the other to re-imagine space with us. Together "we" create a space where everyone is unafraid to speak up and able to explore new avenues in missiological engagements. Transcending binaries and crossing boundaries should not be boring slogans.

Bibliography

Abramson, Anna Jones. "Authors and Others: The Ethics of Inhabiting in J. M. Coetzee's *Elizabeth Costello.*" *Otherness: Essays and Studies* 4 (2014) 21–50.

Abu-Lughod, Lila. "Do Muslim Women Need Saving?" *Time*, November 1, 2013. Online. http://ideas.time.com/2013/11/01/do-muslim-women-need-saving.

Adogame, Afe, and Shobana Shankar, eds. *Religion on the Move! New Dynamics of Religious Expansion in a Globalizing World.* Leiden: Brill, 2013.

Ahmed, Sara. *On Being Included: Racism and Diversity in Institutional Life.* Durham: Duke University Press, 2012.

Ariarajah, S. Wesley. *Not Without My Neighbor: Issues in Interfaith Relations.* Geneva: WCC, 1999.

Asad, Talal. *Genealogies of Religion: Discipline and Reasons of Power in Christianity and Islam.* Baltimore: Johns Hopkins University Press, 1993.

Ashcroft, Bill, Gareth Griffiths, and Helen Tiffin. eds. *The Post-Colonial Studies Reader.* London: Routledge, 2003.

Barnes, Jonathan S. "The Ambivalence of Partnership: A Colonial and Contested History." *Encounter* 74 (2014) 27–44.

Bauer, Laurie, and Peter Trudgill, eds. *Language Myths.* New York: Penguin, 1998.

Berger, Peter. *The Sacred Canopy: Elements of a Sociological Theory of Religion.* New York: Doubleday, 1967.

Berger, Peter, and Thomas Luckmann. *The Social Construction of Reality: A Treatise in the Sociology of Knowledge.* New York: Anchor, 1966.

Beyer, Gerald J. "The Meaning of Solidarity in Catholic Social Teaching." *Political Theology* 15 (2014) 7–25.

Bloom, Irene, trans. *Mencius.* New York: Columbia University Press, 2009.

Bosch, David J. *Transforming Mission: Paradigm Shifts in Theology of Mission.* Maryknoll, NY: Orbis, 1992.

Brockman, David R. *No Longer the Same: Religious Others and the Liberation of Christian Theology.* New York: Palgrave Macmillan, 2011.

Buber, Martin. *I and Thou.* Translated by Ronald Gregor Smith. New York: Scribner Classic, 2000.

Butler, Judith. *The Psychic Life of Power: Theories in Subjection.* Stanford: Stanford University Press, 1997.

Carey, William. *An Enquiry into the Obligations of Christians to Use Means for the Conversion of the Heathens. In Which the Religious State of the Different Nations of the World, the Success of Former Undertakings, and the Practicability of Further Undertakings, Are Considered.* Leicester: Ann Ireland, 1792.

Cardoza-Orlandi, Carlos F., and Justo L. Gonzalez. *To All Nations from All Nations: A History of the Christian Missionary Movement.* Nashville: Abingdon, 2013.

Cash, W. Wilson. "The Jerusalem Meeting of the International Missionary Council." *The Churchman* 42.4 (1928) 269–77. Online. https://biblicalstudies.org.uk/pdf/churchman/042-04_269.pdf.

Chomsky, Noam. *Language and Mind.* Cambridge: Cambridge University Press, 2006.

Chow, Rey. *Not Like a Native Speaker: On Languaging as a Postcolonial Experience.* New York: Columbia University Press, 2014.

Cleall, Esme. *Missionary Discourses of Difference: Negotiating Otherness in the British Empire, 1840–1900.* New York: Palgrave Macmillan, 2012.

Cleveland, Christena. *Disunity in Christ: Uncovering the Hidden Forces That Keep Us Apart.* Downers Grove, IL: InterVarsity, 2013.

Cooper-White, Pamela. *Braided Selves: Collected Essays on Multiplicity, God and Persons.* Eugene, OR: Cascade, 2011.

Cox, Harvey. *The Future of Faith.* New York: HarperOne, 2010.

Cushman, Philip. *Constructing the Self, Constructing America: A Cultural History of Psychotherapy.* Cambridge, MA: Da Capo, 1995.

Dabashi, Hamid. *Can Non-Europeans Think?* London: Zed, 2015.

De Kock, Leon. *Civilising Barbarians: Missionary Narrative and African Textual Response in Nineteenth-Century South Africa.* Johannesburg: Witwatersrand University Press, 1996.

Denny, Frederick M., and Rodney L. Taylor, eds. *The Holy Book in Comparative Perspective.* Columbia: University of South Carolina Press, 1985.

Derrida, Jacques. *Monolingualism of the Other or The Prosthesis of Origin.* Translated by Patrick Mensah. Standford: Standford University Press, 1998.

Dharmaraj, Jacob S. *Colonialism and Christian Mission: Postcolonial Reflections.* Delhi: ISPCK, 1993.

Downes, William. *Language and Religion: A Journey into the Human Mind.* Cambridge: Cambridge University Press, 2011.

Enegho, Felix Ehimare, and Friday John Imaekhai. "Language and Christian Evangelism in a Pluralistic Society: The Nigerian Model." *Swedish Missiological Themes* 96 (2008) 339–48.

Fanon, Frantz. *Black Skin, White Masks.* New York: Grove, 1967.

Foucault, Michel. *Discipline & Punish: The Birth of the Prison.* Translated by Alan Sheridan. 2nd ed. New York: Vintage, 1995.

———. *Power/Knowledge: Selected Interviews and Other Writings, 1972–1977.* Edited by Colin Gordon. Translated by Colin Gordon et al. New York: Pantheon, 1980.

Fowl, Stephen E., ed. *The Theological Interpretation of Scripture: Classic and Contemporary Readings.* Malden, MA: Blackwell, 1997.

Francis. *The Name of God Is Mercy.* Translated by Oonagh Stransky. New York: Random, 2016.

Freeman, Mark. *The Priority of the Other: Thinking and Living Beyond the Self.* New York: Oxford University Press, 2014.

Freire, Paulo. *Education for Critical Consciousness*. New York: Bloomsbury Academic, 2016.

Galli, Mark. "Missions and Ecumenism: John R. Mott." *Christianity Today* 65 (2000). Online. http://www.christianitytoday.com/history/issues/issue-65/missions-and-ecumenism-john-r-mott.html.

Gee, James Paul. *Social Linguistics and Literacies: Ideology in Discourse*. 4th ed. New York: Routledge, 2012.

Geertz, Clifford. *Local Knowledge: Further Essays in Interpretive Anthropology*. New York: Basic, 1983.

Gergen, Kenneth J. *Relational Being: Beyond Self and Community*. New York: Oxford University Press, 2009.

González, Justo L. *The Changing Shape of Church History*. St. Louis: Chalice, 2002.

Grau, Marion. *Rethinking Mission in the Postcolony: Salvation, Society, and Subversion*. New York: T&T Clark, 2011.

Green, Nile, and Mary Searle-Chatterjee, eds. *Religion, Language, and Power*. New York: Routledge, 2008.

Griffiths, Paul J., ed. *Christianity through Non-Christian Eyes*. Maryknoll, NY: Orbis, 2004.

Gunton, Colin E., ed. *The Theology of Reconciliation*. London: T&T Clark, 2003.

Harries, Jim, and Fred Lewis. "Is Mission Diverse, or Is It All Just Money? An Examination of Western Mission to Africa." *Evangelical Review of Theology* 36 (2012) 347–55.

Hayward, Victor E. W. "The World Council's Fourth Assembly." *The Ecumenical Review* 19 (1967) 48–58.

Heim, S. Mark. "Mission and Dialogue: 50 Years after Tambaram." *The Christian Century* 105.11 (1988) 341–43.

Hermans, Chris A. M., et al, eds. *Social Constructionism and Theology*. Lieden: Brill, 2002.

Heschel, Abraham Joshua. *Man Is Not Alone: A Philosophy of Religion*. New York: Farrar, Straus, and Giroux, 1976.

Hiebert, Paul G. *Anthropological Insights for Missionaries*. Grand Rapids: Baker, 1985.

———. *Anthropological Reflections on Missiological Issues*. Grand Rapids: Baker, 1994.

———. *The Gospel in Human Contexts: Anthropological Explorations for Contemporary Missions*. Grand Rapids: Baker Academic, 2009.

———. *The Missiological Implications of Epistemological Shifts: Affirming Truth in a Modern/Postmodern World*. Harrisburg, PA: Trinity, 1999.

"How English Evolved into a Global Language." *BBC News*, December 20, 2010. Online. http://www.bbc.com/news/magazine-12017753.

Howell, Brian M. *Short-Term Mission: An Ethnography of Christian Travel Narrative and Experience*. Downers Grove, IL: IVP Academic, 2012.

Huntington, Samuel P. "The Clash of Civilizations?" *Foreign Affairs* 72 (1993) 22–49.

Illich, Ivan. "To Hell with Good Intentions." Address delivered to the Conference on InterAmerican Student Projects (CIASP), Cuernavaca, Mexico, April 20, 1968. Online. http://www.swaraj.org/illich_hell.htm.

Irigaray, Luce. *To Speak Is Never Neutral*. New York: Continuum, 2002.

Isherwood, Lisa, and David Harris. *Radical Otherness: Sociological and Theological Approaches*. Gender, Theology, and Spirituality. Durham, UK: Acumen, 2013.

Jenkins, Philip. *The Lost History of Christianity: The Thousand-Year Golden Age of the Church in the Middle East, Africa, and Asia—and How It Died*. New York: HarperCollins, 2008.

Jensen, David H. *In the Company of Others: A Dialogical Christology*. Cleveland: Pilgrim, 2001.

Jenson, Matt, and David Wilhite. *The Church: A Guide for the Perplexed*. London: T&T Clark, 2010.

Jeung, Russell. *At Home in Exile: Finding Jesus among My Ancestors and Refugee Neighbors*. Grand Rapids: Zondervan, 2016.

John Paul II. *Encyclical Letter Redemptoris Missio of the Supreme Pontiff John Paul II on the Permanent Validity of the Church's Missionary Mandate*. Washington, DC: Catholic Conference, 1990.

Kane, Ross. "Tragedies of Communion: Seeking Reconciliation amid Colonial Legacies." *The Anglican Theological Review* 97 (2015) 391–412.

Keane, Webb. *Christian Moderns: Freedom and Fetish in the Mission Encounter*. Berkeley: University of California Press, 2007.

Keum, Jooseop. "An Introduction to the New WCC Mission Statement." *Swedish Missiological Themes* 101 (2013) 291–300.

Khobnya, Svetlana. "Reconciliation Must Prevail. A Fresh Look at 2 Corinthians 5:14–6:2." *European Journal of Theology* 25 (2016) 128–36.

Koyama, Kosuke. "Rejoice in Hope." In *Together on the Way: Official Report of the Eighth Assembly of the World Council of Churches*, edited by Diane Kessler, 38–41. Geneva: WCC, 1999.

LaHurd, Carol Schersten, Darrell Jadock, and Kathryn Mary Lohre, eds. *Engaging Others, Knowing Ourselves: A Lutheran Calling in a Multi-religious World*. Minneapolis: Lutheran University Press, 2016.

Landry, Donna, and Gerald MacLean, eds. *The Spivak Reader: Selected Works of Gayati Chakravorty Spivak*. London: Routledge, 1996.

Lausanne Movement. "Cape Town 2010: The Third Lausanne Congress on World Evangelization." *Lausanne Movement*, October 24, 2010. Online. https://www.lausanne.org/gatherings/congress/cape-town-2010-3.

Lee, Byungohk. "A Missional Hermeneutic of the Other: A Dialogue between Levinas and Confucianism." *Missiology: An International Review* 41 (2013) 416–26.

Lefever, Ernest W. *Amsterdam to Nairobi: The World Council of Churches and the Third World*. Washington, DC: Ethics and Public Policy Center, 1979.

Leitch, Vincent B., ed. *The Norton Anthology of Theory and Criticism*. 2nd ed. New York: Norton, 2010.

Levi-Strauss, Claude. *The Savage Mind*. Chicago: University of Chicago Press, 1966.

Levinas, Emmaneul. *Otherwise Than Being, Or, Beyond Essence*. Translated by Alphonso Lingis. The Hague: M Nijhoff, 1981.

———. *Totality and Infinity: An Essay on Exteriority*. Translated by Alphonso Lingis. Dordrecht: Kluwer Academic, 1979.

Lindbeck, George A. "An Interview with George Lindbeck: Performing the Faith." *The Christian Century* (1996) 28–35.

———. *The Nature of Doctrine: Religion and Theology in a Postliberal Age*. Philadelphia: Westminster, 1984.

Liu, Shu-hsien. "Confucianism as World Philosophy: A Response to Neville's Boston Confucianism from a Neo-Confucian Perspective." *Journal of Ecumenical Studies* 40 (2003) 59–73.

Logan, Carolyn, ed. *Counterbalance: Gendered Perspectives on Writing and Language.* Peterborough, ON: Broadview, 1996.

Ma, Wonsuk, and Julie C. Ma, eds. *Asian Church and God's Mission: Studies Presented in the International Symposium on Asian Mission in Manila, January 2002.* Manila: OMF Literature, 2003.

Macedo, Donaldo, Bessie Dendrinos, and Panayota Gounari. *The Hegemony of English.* Boulder, CO: Paradigm, 2003.

Marty, Martin. *October 31, 1517: Martin Luther and the Day that Changed the World.* Brewster, MA: Paraclete, 2016.

McGee, Gary B. "Shortcut to Language Preparation? Radical Evangelicals, Missions, and the Gift of Tongues." *International Bulletin of Missionary Research* 25 (2001) 118–23.

McGuire, Meredith B. *Lived Religion: Faith and Practice in Everyday Life.* New York: Oxford University Press, 2008.

McWhorter, John. *The Power of Babel: A Natural History of Language.* New York: Times Books, 2001.

Miyamoto, Ken Christoph. *God's Mission in Asia: A Comparative and Contextual Study of This-Worldly Holiness and the Theology of Missio Dei in M. M. Thomas and C. S. Song.* Eugene, OR: Pickwick, 2007.

Myers, Bryant L. *Walking with the Poor: Principles and Practices of Transformational Development.* Maryknoll, NY: Orbis, 2011.

Nandy, Ashis. *The Intimate Enemy: Loss and Recovery of Self under Colonialism.* Delhi: Oxford University Press, 1983.

Nessan, Craig L. "The Cross as Foundation for the Ministry of Reconciliation: Ending Violence in Our Endangered Globe." *Currents in Theology and Mission* 40 (2013) 95–105.

———. *Shalom Church: The Body of Christ as Ministering Community.* Minneapolis: Fortress, 2010.

Netland, Harold A. *Dissonant Voices: Religious Pluralism & the Question of Truth.* Vancouver: Regent College Publishing, 1999.

Neusner, Jacob, Ernest S. Frerichs, and Caroline McCracken-Flesher, eds. *"To See Ourselves as Others See Us": Christians, Jews, "Others" in Late Antiquity.* Chico, CA: Scholars, 1985.

Newbigin, Lesslie. *Signs Amid the Rubble: The Purposes of God in Human History.* Edited by Geoffrey Wainwright. Grand Rapids: Eerdmans, 2003.

Niles, Preman. *From East and West: Rethinking Christian Mission.* St. Louis: Chalice, 2004.

Nussbaum, Martha C. *Hiding from Humanity: Disgust, Shame, and the Law.* Princeton: Princeton University Press, 2004.

Ogden, Thomas H. *Reverie and Interpretation: Sensing Something Human.* London: Karnac, 1999.

Olson, Gary A., and Lynn Worsham, eds. *Race, Rhetoric, and the Postcolonial.* Albany: State University of New York Press, 1999.

Oppenheim, Michael. "*Langue, Parole, et Chanson*: On Language as Song in Psychoanalysis and Jewish Philosophy." *Pastoral Psychology* 62 (2013) 403–21.

Ott, Craig, Stephen J. Strauss, and Timothy C. Tennent. *Encountering Theology of Mission: Biblical Foundations, Historical Developments, and Contemporary Issues.* Grand Rapids: Baker Academic, 2010.

Pagels, Elaine. *The Origin of Satan.* New York: Random, 1995.

Panikkar, Raimon. *The Rhythm of Being: The Unbroken Trinity.* Gifford Lectures 1989–90. Maryknoll, NY: Orbis, 2013.

———. *The Trinity and the Religious Experience of Man.* Maryknoll, NY: Orbis, 1973.

Paul VI. *The Declaration on the Relation of the Church to Non-Christian Religions.* Glen Rock, NJ: Paulist, 1966.

Peters, Rebecca Todd. *Solidarity Ethics: Transformation in a Globalized World.* Minneapolis: Fortress, 2014.

Pierce, Andrew J. "Authentic Identities." *Social Theory and Practice* 41 (2015) 435–57.

Pontifical Council for Interreligious Dialogue. "Dialogue and Proclamation." May 19, 1991. Online. www.vatican.va/roman_curia/pontifical_councils/interelg/documents/rc_pc_interelg_doc_19051991_dialogue-and-proclamatio_en.html.

Rajashekar, Paul. "Faith and the Other: Theological Perspectives." *Currents in Theology and Mission* 24 (1997) 430–38.

Ricoeur, Paul. *Oneself as Another.* Chicago: University of Chicago Press, 1992.

Rieger, Joerg. "Theology and Mission between Neocolonialism and Postcolonialism." *Mission Studies* 21 (2004) 201–27.

Robinson, Gnana, ed. *For the Sake of the Gospel: Essays in Honour of Samuel Amirtham.* Madurai: TTS, 1980.

Rynkiewich, Michael A. *Soul, Self, and Society: A Postmodern Anthropology for Mission in a Postcolonial World.* Eugene, OR: Cascade, 2011.

Said, Edward W. *Culture and Imperialism.* New York: Vintage, 1993.

———. *Orientalism.* New York: Vintage, 1994.

———. *The World, the Text, and the Critic.* Cambridge, MA: Harvard University Press, 1983.

Samartha, Stanley. *Between Two Cultures: Ecumenical Ministry in a Pluralist World.* Geneva: WCC, 1996.

———. *One Christ, Many Religions: Toward a Revised Christology.* Maryknoll, NY: Orbis, 2000.

Sanneh, Lamin. *Translating the Message.* 2nd ed. Maryknoll, NY: Orbis, 2009.

———. *Whose Religion Is Christianity? The Gospel Beyond the West.* Grand Rapids: Eerdmans, 2003.

Saussure, Ferdinand de. *Course in General Linguistics.* Edited by Charles Bally and Albert Sechehaye with Albert Riedlinger. New York: McGraw Hill, 1966.

Scott, Peter, and William T. Cavanaugh, eds. *The Blackwell Companion to Political Theology.* Malden, MA: Blackwell, 2004.

Searle, John. *The Construction of Social Reality.* New York: Free Press, 1995.

———. *Making the Social World: The Structure of Human Civilization.* Oxford: Oxford University Press, 2010.

Sebastian, J. Jayakiran. "Believing and Belonging: Secularism and Religion in India." *International Review of Mission* 92 (2003) 204–11.

Second Vatican Council. "Ad Gentes." December 7, 1965. Online. http://www.vatican.va/archive/hist_councils/ii_vatican_council/documents/vat-ii_decree_19651207_ad-gentes_en.html

Sen, Amartya. *Identity and Violence: The Illusion of Destiny.* New York: Norton, 2006.

Smart, Ninian. *Worldviews: Crosscultural Explorations of Human Beliefs.* Englewood Cliffs, NJ: Prentice Hall, 1995.

Smith, Jonathan Z. *Relating Religion: Essays in the Study of Religion.* Chicago: University of Chicago Press, 2004.

Smith, Wilfred Cantwell. *The Meaning and End of Religion.* Minneapolis: Fortress, 1991.

Song, C. S. *Tracing the Footsteps of God: Discovering What You Really Believe.* Minneapolis: Fortress, 2007.

Stanley, Brian. *The World Missionary Conference, Edinburgh 1910.* Grand Rapids: Eerdmans, 2009.

Storrar, William F., Peter J. Casarella, and Paul Louis Metzger, eds. *A World for All? Global Civil Society in Political Theory and Trinitarian Theology.* Grand Rapids: Eerdmans, 2011.

Storrar, William F., and Andrew R. Morton, eds. *Public Theology for the Twenty-First Century: Essays in Honour of Duncan B. Forrester.* New York: T&T Clark, 2003.

Suarez, Debra. "The Paradox of Linguistic Hegemony and the Maintenance of Spanish as a Heritage Language in the United States." *Journal of Multilingual and Multicultural Development* 23 (2002) 512–30.

Sugirtharajah, R. S. *The Bible and the Third World: Precolonial, Colonial, and Postcolonial Encounters.* Cambridge: Cambridge University Press, 2001.

———. *Exploring Postcolonial Biblical Criticism: History, Method, Practice.* Malden, MA: Wiley-Blackwell, 2012.

———, ed. *The Postcolonial Biblical Reader.* Malden, MA: Blackwell, 2006.

Tan, Jonathan Y. "Missio inter gentes: Towards a New Paradigm in the Mission Theology of the Federation of Asian Bishop's Conference (FABC)." *Mission Studies* 21 (2004) 65–95.

Taylor, Charles. *The Ethics of Authenticity.* Cambridge, MA: Harvard University Press, 1991.

Thiong'o, Ngũgĩ wa. *Decolonising the Mind: The Politics of Language in African Literature.* London: Currey, 1986.

Thomas, M. M. "The Absoluteness of Jesus Christ and Christ-Centered Syncretism." *Ecumenical Review* 37 (1985) 387–97.

———. "An Assessment of Tambaram's Contribution to the Search of the Asian Churches for an Authentic Selfhood." *International Review of Mission* 77 (1988) 390–97.

Thomas, T. Jacob, ed. *M. M. Thomas Reader: Selected Texts on Theology, Religion, and Society.* Tiruvalla, India: Christava Sahitya Samithy, 2002.

Thuesen, Peter J. "George Lindbeck on Truth." *Lutheran Quarterly* 10 (1996) 47–58.

Tinker, George. *American Indian Liberation: A Theology of Sovereignty.* Maryknoll, NY: Orbis, 2008.

Treat, James, ed. *Native and Christian: Indigenous Voices on Religious Identity in the United States and Canada.* New York: Routledge, 1996.

Tutu, Desmond. *God Has a Dream.* New York: Image, Doubleday, 2004.

Van Voorst, Robert E. *Anthology of World Scriptures.* 6th ed. Belmont, CA: Thomson Wadsworth, 2008.

Vatican. "The Pontifical Council for Interreligious Dialogue." June 28, 1988. Online. http://www.vatican.va/roman_curia/pontifical_councils/interelg/documents/rc_pc_interelg_pro_20051996_en.html.

Volf, Miroslav. *Exclusion & Embrace: A Theological Exploration of Identity, Otherness, and Reconciliation*. Nashville: Abingdon, 1996.

Vos, Pieter, and Onno Zijlstra, eds. *The Law of God: Exploring God and Civilization*. Studies in Reformed Theology 28. Lieden: Brill, 2014.

Waskow, Arthur. "The Torah of Esau and Jacob, Gaza and Israel." *Shalom Center*, November 26, 2012. Online. https://theshalomcenter.org/torah-esau-and-jacob-gaza-and-israel.

Watts, Alan W. *The Way of Zen*. New York: Vintage, 1989.

Weiming, Tu, and Daisaku Ikeda. *New Horizons in Eastern Humanism: Buddhism, Confucianism, and the Quest for Global Peace*. New York: IB Tauris, 2011.

Welch, Sharon D. *After Empire: The Art and Ethos of Enduring Peace*. Minneapolis: Fortress, 2004.

World Council of Churches (WCC). "Guidelines for Dialogue and Relations with People of Other Religions." September 2, 2002. Online. https://www.oikoumene.org/en/resources/documents/central-committee/2002/guidelines-for-dialogue-and-relations-with-people-of-other-religions.

———. "Guidelines on Dialogue with People of Living Faiths and Ideology." February 1, 2010. Online. https://www.oikoumene.org/en/resources/documents/wcc-programmes/interreligious-dialogue-and-cooperation/interreligious-trust-and-respect/guidelines-on-dialogue-with-people-of-living-faiths-and-ideologies.

———. "History." Online. https://www.oikoumene.org/en/what-we-do/cwme/history.

———. "Statement on the Middle East." August 10, 1983. Online. https://www.oikoumene.org/en/resources/documents/assembly/1983-vancouver/statement-on-the-middle-east.

World Missionary Conference. *Report of Commission I: Carrying the Gospel to All the Non-Christian World*. Edinburgh: World Missionary Conference, 1910.

Yong, Amos, and Clifton Clarke, eds. *Global Renewal, Religious Pluralism, and the Great Commission: Towards a Renewal Theology of Mission and Interreligious Encounter*. Lexington, KY: Emeth, 2011.

Ziehl, Nell. "Coping with Narcissistic Personality Disorder in the White House." *Quartz Media*, December 6, 2016. Online. https://qz.com/852187/coping-with-chaos-in-the-white-house.

Zizioulas, John D. *Communion and Otherness: Further Studies in Personhood and the Church*. Edited by Paul McPartlan. London: T&T Clark, 2006.

Zondag, Hessel J. "Just Like Other People: Narcissism among Pastors." *Pastoral Psychology* 52 (2004) 423–37.

Index